Famous Men of the Middle Ages

By John Haaren, LL.D., District Superintendent of Schools The City of New York,

and

A. B. Poland, Ph.D. Superintendent of Schools Newark N.J.

Printed in Scotts Valley, CA – USA.

Haaren, John and Poland, A. B.

Famous Men of the Middle Ages / John Haaren and A. B. Poland – 1st ed.

1. History 2. Middle Ages

PREFACE

The study of history, like the study of a landscape, should begin with the most conspicuous features. Not until these have been fixed in memory will the lesser features fall into their appropriate places and assume their right proportions.

The famous men of ancient and modern times are the mountain peaks of history. It is logical then that the study of history should begin with the biographies of these men.

Not only is it logical; it is also pedagogical. Experience has proven that in order to attract and hold the child's attention each conspicuous feature of history presented to him should have an individual for its center. The child identifies himself with the personage presented. It is not Romulus or Hercules or Cæsar or Alexander that the child has in mind when he reads, but himself, acting under similar conditions.

Prominent educators, appreciating these truths, have long recognized the value of biography as a preparation for the study of history and have given it an important place in their scheme of studies.

The former practice in many elementary schools of beginning the detailed study of American history without any previous knowledge of general history limited the pupil's range of vision, restricted his sympathies, and left him without material for comparisons. Moreover, it denied to him a knowledge of his inheritance from the Greek philosopher, the Roman lawgiver, the Teutonic lover of freedom. Hence the recommendation so strongly urged in the report of the Committee of Ten--and emphasized, also, in the report of the Committee of Fifteen--that the study of Greek, Roman and modern European history in the form of biography should precede the study of detailed American history in our elementary schools. The Committee of Ten recommends an eight years' course in history, beginning with the fifth year in school and continuing to the end of the high school course. The first two years of this course are given wholly to the study of biography and mythology. The Committee of fifteen recommends that history be taught in all the grades of the elementary school and emphasizes the value of biography and of general history.

The series of historical stories to which this volume belongs was prepared in conformity with the foregoing recommendations and with the best practice of leading schools. It has been the aim of the authors to make an interesting story of each man's life and to tell these stories in a style so simple that pupils in the lower grades will read them with pleasure, and so dignified that they may be used with profit as text-books for reading.

Teachers who find it impracticable to give to the study of mythology and biography a place of its own in an already overcrowded curriculum usually prefer to correlate history with reading and for this purpose the volumes of this series will be found most desirable.

The value of the illustrations can scarcely be over-estimated. They will be found to surpass in number and excellence anything heretofore offered in a school-book. For the most part they are reproductions of world-famous pictures, and for that reason the artists' names are generally affixed.

CONTENTS

INTRODUCTION

The Gods of the Teutons

In the little volume called *The Famous Men of Rome* you have read about the great empire which the Romans established. Now we come to a time when the power of Rome was broken and tribes of barbarians who lived north of the Danube and the Rhine took possession of lands that had been part of the Roman Empire. These tribes were the Goths, Vandals, Huns, Franks and Anglo-Saxons. From them have come the greatest nations of modern times. All except the Huns belonged to the same race and are known as Teutons. They were war-like, savage and cruel. They spoke the same language--though in different dialects--and worshiped the same gods. Like the old Greeks and Romans they had many gods.

Woden, who was also called Odin, was the greatest of all. His name means "mighty warrior," and he was king of all the gods. He rode through the air mounted on Sleipnir, an eightfooted horse fleeter than the eagle. When the tempest roared the Teutons said it was the snorting of Sleipnir. When their ships came safely into port they said it was Woden's breath that had filled their sails and wafted their vessels over the blue waters.

Thor, a son of Woden, ranked next to him among the gods. He rode through the air in a chariot drawn by goats. The Germans called him Donar and Thunar, words which are like our word thunder. From this we can see that he was the thunder god. In his hand he carried a wonderful hammer which always came back to his hand when he threw it. Its head was so bright that as it flew through the air it made the lightning. When it struck the vast ice mountains they reeled and splintered into fragments, and thus Thor's hammer made thunder.

Another great god of our ancestors was Tiew. He was a son of Woden and was the god of battle. He was armed with a sword which flashed like lightning when he brandished it. A savage chief named Attila routed the armies of the Romans and so terrified all the world that he was called "The Scourge of God." His people believed that he gained his victories because he had the sword of Tiew, which a herdsman chanced to find where the god had allowed it to fall. The Teutons prayed to Tiew when they went into battle.

Fig 1. Thor and Hymir go fishing for the Midgard Serpent. From a 18th century Icelandic manuscript.

Frija (free' ya) was the wife of Woden and the queen of the gods. She ruled the bright clouds that gleam in the summer sky, and caused them to pour their showers on meadow and forest and mountain.

Four of the days of the week are named after these gods. Tuesday means the day of Tiew; Wednesday, the day of Woden; Thursday, the day of Thor; and Friday, the day of Frija.

Frija's son was Baldur; who was the favorite of all the gods. Only Loki, the spirit of evil, hated him. Baldur's face was as bright as sunshine. His hair gleamed like burnished gold. Wherever he went night was turned into day.

One morning when he looked toward earth from his father Woden's palace black clouds covered the sky, but he saw a splendid rainbow reaching down from the clouds to the earth. Baldur walked upon this rainbow from the home of the gods to the dwellings of men. The rainbow was a bridge upon which the gods used to come to earth.

When Baldur stepped from the rainbow-bridge to the earth he saw a king's daughter so beautiful that he fell in love with her.

But an earthly prince had also fallen in love with her. So he and Baldur fought for her hand. Baldur was a god and hence was very much stronger than the prince. But some of Baldur's magic food was given to the prince and it made him as strong as Baldur.

Frija heard about this and feared that Baldur was doomed to be killed. So she went to every beast on the land and every fish of the sea and every bird of the air and to every tree of the wood and every plant of the field and made each promise not to hurt Baldur.

But she forgot the mistletoe. So Loki, who always tried to do mischief, made an arrow of mistletoe, and gave it to the prince who shot and killed Baldur with it.

Then all the gods wept, the summer breeze wailed, the leaves fell from the sorrowing trees, the flowers faded and died from grief, and the earth grew stiff and cold. Bruin, the bear, and his neighbors, the hedgehogs and squirrels, crept into holes and refused to eat for weeks and weeks.

The pleasure of all living things in Baldur's presence means the happiness that the sunlight brings. The sorrow of all living things at his death means the gloom of northern countries when winter comes.

The Valkyries were beautiful female warriors. They had some of Woden's own strength and were armed with helmet and shield and spear. Like Woden, they rode unseen through the air and their horses were almost as swift as Sleipnir himself. They swiftly carried Woden's favorite warriors to Valhalla, the hall of the slain. The walls of Valhalla were hung with shields; its ceiling glittered with polished spearheads. From its five hundred and forty gates, each wide enough for eight hundred men abreast to march through, the warriors rushed every morning to fight a battle that lasted till nightfall and began again at the break of each day. When the heroes returned to Valhalla the Valkyries served them with goblets of mead such as Woden drank himself.

The Teutons believed that before there were any gods or any world there was a great empty space where the world now is. It was called by the curious name Ginnungagap, which means a yawning abyss.

To the north of Ginnungagap it was bitterly cold. Nothing was there but fields of snow and mountains of ice. To the south of Ginnungagap was a region where frost and snow were never seen. It was always bright, and was the home of light and heat. The sunshine from the South melted the ice mountains of the North so that they toppled over and fell into Ginnungagap. There they were changed into a frost giant whose name was Ymir (e'mir). He had three sons. They and their father were so strong that the gods were afraid of them.

So Woden and his brothers killed Ymir. They broke his body in pieces and made the world of them. His bones and teeth became mountains and rocks; his hair became leaves for trees and plants; out of his skull was made the sky.

But Ymir was colder than ice, and the earth that was made of his body was so cold that nothing could live or grow upon it. So the gods took sparks from the home of light and set them in the sky. Two big ones were the sun and moon and the little ones were the stars. Then the earth became warm. Trees grew and flowers bloomed, so that the world was a beautiful home for men.

Of all the trees the most wonderful was a great ash tree, sometimes called the "world tree." Its branches covered the earth and reached beyond the sky till they almost touched the stars. Its roots ran in three directions, to heaven, to the frost giants' home and to the under-world, beneath the earth.

Near the roots in the dark under-world sat the Norns, or fates. Each held a bowl with which she dipped water out of a sacred spring and poured it upon the roots of the ash tree. This was the reason why this wonderful tree was always growing, and why it grew as high as the sky.

When Woden killed Ymir he tried to kill all Ymir's children too; but one escaped, and ever after he and his family, the frost giants, tried to do mischief, and fought against gods and men.

According to the belief of the Teutons these wicked giants will some day destroy the beautiful world. Even the gods themselves will be killed in a dreadful battle with them. First of all will come three terrible winters without any spring or summer. The sun and moon will cease to shine and the bright stars will fall from the sky. The earth will be shaken as when there is a great earthquake; the waves of the sea will roar and the highest mountains will totter and fall. The trees will be torn up by the roots, and even the "world tree" will tremble from its roots to its topmost boughs. At last the quivering earth will sink beneath the waters of the sea.

Then Loki, the spirit of evil, will break loose from the fetters with which the gods have bound him. The frost giants will join him. They will try to make a secret attack on the gods. But Heimdall, the sentry of heaven, will be on guard at the end of the rainbow-bridge. He needs no more sleep than a bird and can see for a hundred miles either by day or night. He only can sound the horn whose blast can be heard through heaven and earth and the under-world. Loki and his army will be seen by him. His loud alarm will sound and bring the gods together. They will rush to meet the giants. Woden will wield his spear--Tiew his glittering sword--Thor his terrible hammer. These will all be in vain. The gods must die. But so must the giants and Loki.

And then a new earth will rise from the sea. The leaves of its forests will never fall; its fields will yield harvests unsown. And in a hall far brighter than Woden's Valhalla the brave and good will be gathered forever.

The Nibelungs

1

The time came when the people of Western Europe learned to believe in one God and were converted to Christianity, but the old stories about the gods and Valkyries and giants and heroes, who were half gods and half men, were not forgotten.

These stories were repeated from father to son for generations, and in the twelfth century a poet, whose name we do not know, wrote them in verse. He called his poem the Nibelungenlied (song of the Nibelungs). It is the great national poem of the Germans. The legends told in it are the basis of Wagner's operas.

"Nibelungs" was the name given to some northern dwarfs whose king had once possessed a great treasure of gold and precious stones but had lost it. Whoever got possession of this treasure was followed by a curse. The Nibelungenlied tells the adventures of those who possessed the treasure.

2

In the grand old city of Worms, in Burgundy, there lived long ago the princess Kriemhilda. Her eldest brother Gunther was king of Burgundy.

And in the far-away Netherlands, where the Rhine pours its waters into the sea, dwelt a prince named Siegfried, son of Siegmund, the king.

Ere long Sir Siegfried heard of the beauty of fair Kriemhilda. He said to his father, "Give me twelve knights and I will ride to King Gunther's land. I must win the heart of Kriemhilda."

After seven days' journey the prince and his company drew near to the gates of Worms. All wondered who the strangers were and whence they came. Hagen, Kriemhilda's uncle, guessed. He said, "I never have seen the famed hero of Netherlands, yet I am sure that yonder knight is none but Sir Siegfried."

"And who," asked the wondering people, "may Siegfried be?"

"Siegfried," answered Sir Hagen, "is a truly wonderful knight. Once when riding all alone, he came to a mountain where lay the treasure of the king of the Nibelungs. The king's two sons had brought it out from the cave in which it had been hidden, to divide it between them. But they did not agree about the division. So when Seigfied drew near both princes said, 'Divide for us, Sir Siegfried, our father's hoard.' There were so many jewels that one hundred wagons could not carry them, and of ruddy gold there was even more. Seigfied made the fairest division he could, and as a reward the princes gave him their father's sword called Balmung. But although Siegfried had done his best to satisfy them with his division, they soon fell to quarreling and fighting, and when he tried to separate them they made an attack on him. To save his own life he slew them both. Alberich, a mountain dwarf, who had long been guardian of the Nibelung hoard, rushed to avenge his masters; but Siegfried vanquished him and took from him his cap of darkness which made its wearer invisible and gave him the strength of twelve men. The hero then ordered Alberich to place the treasure again in the mountain cave and guard it for him."

Hagen then told another story of Siegfried:

"Once he slew a fierce dragon and bathed himself in its blood, and this turned the hero's skin to horn, so that no sword or spear can wound him."

When Hagen had told these tales he advised King Gunther and the people of Burgundy to receive Siegfried with all honor.

So, as the fashion was in those times, games were held in the courtyard of the palace in honor of Siegfried, and Kriemhilda watched the sport from her window.

For a full year Siegfried stayed at the court of King Gunther, but never in all that time told why he had come and never once saw Kriemhilda.

At the end of the year sudden tidings came that the Saxons and Danes, as was their habit, were pillaging the lands of Burgundy. At the head of a thousand Burgundian knights Siegfried conquered both Saxons and Danes. The king of the Danes was taken prisoner and the Saxon king surrendered.

The victorious warriors returned to Worms and the air was filled with glad shouts of welcome. King Gunther asked Kriemhilda to welcome Siegfried and offer him the thanks of all the land of Burgundy.

Siegfried stood before her, and she said, "Welcome, Sir Siegfried, welcome; we thank you one and all." He bent before her and she kissed him.

3

Far over the sea from sunny Burgundy lived Brunhilda, queen of Iceland. Fair was she of face and strong beyond compare. If a knight would woo and win her he must surpass her in three contests: leaping, hurling the spear and pitching the stone. If he failed in even one, he must forfeit his life.

King Gunther resolved to wed this strange princess and Siegfried promised to help him. "But," said Siegfried, "if we succeed, I must have as my wife thy sister Kriemhilda." To this

Gunther agreed, and the voyage to Iceland began.

When Gunther and his companions neared Brunhilda's palace the gates were opened and the strangers were welcomed.

Siegfried thanked the queen for her kindness and told how Gunther had come to Iceland in hope of winning her hand.

"If in three contests he gain the mastery," she said, "I will become his wife. If not, both he and you who are with him must lose your lives."

Brunhilda prepared for the contests. Her shield was so thick and heavy that four strong men were needed to bear it. Three could scarcely carry her spear and the stone that she hurled could just be lifted by twelve.

Siegfried now helped Gunther in a wonderful way. He put on his cap of darkness, so that no one could see him. Then he stood by Gunther's side and did the fighting. Brunhilda threw her spear against the kings bright shield and sparks flew from the steel. But the unseen knight dealt Brunhilda such blows that she confessed herself conquered.

In the second and third contests she fared no better, and so she had to become King Gunther's bride. But she said that before she would leave Iceland she must tell all her kinsmen. Daily her kinsfolk came riding to the castle, and soon an army had assembled.

Then Gunther and his friends feared unfair play. So Siegfried put on his cap of darkness, stepped into a boat, and went to the Nibelung land where Alberich the dwarf was guarding the wonderful Nibelung treasure.

"Bring me here," he cried to the dwarf, "a thousand Nibelung knights." At the call of the dwarf the warriors gathered around Sir Siegfried. Then they sailed with him to Brunhilda's isle and the queen and her kinsmen, fearing such warriors, welcomed them instead of fighting. Soon after their arrival King Gunther and his men, Siegfried and his Nibelungs, and Queen Brunhilda, with two thousand of her kinsmen set sail for King Gunther's land.

As soon as they reached Worms the marriage of Gunther and Brunhilda took place. Siegfried and Kriemhilda also were married, and after their marriage went to Siegfried's Netherlands castle. There they lived more happily than I can tell.

4

Now comes the sad part of the Nibelung tale.

Brunhilda and Gunther invited Siegfried and Kriemhilda to visit them at Worms. During the visit the two queens quarreled and Brunhilda made Gunther angry with Siegfried. Hagen, too, began to hate Siegfried and wished to kill him.

But Siegfried could not be wounded except in one spot on which a falling leaf had rested when he bathed himself in the dragon's blood. Only Kriemhilda knew where this spot was. Hagen told her to sew a little silk cross upon Siegfried's dress to mark the spot, so that he might defend Siegfried in a fight.

No battle was fought, but Siegfried went hunting with Gunther and Hagen one day and they challenged him to race with them. He easily won, but after running he was hot and thirsty and knelt to drink at a spring. Then Hagen seized a spear and plunged it through the cross into the hero's body. Thus the treasure of the Nibelungs brought disaster to Siegfried.

Gunther and Hagen told Kriemhilda that robbers in the wood had slain her husband, but she could not be deceived.

Kriemhilda determined to take vengeance on the murderers of Siegfried, and so she would not leave Worms. There, too, stayed one thousand knights who had followed Siegfried from the Nibelung land.

Soon after Siegfried's death Kriemhilda begged her younger brother to bring the Nibelung treasure from the mountain cave to Worms.

When it arrived Kriemhilda gave gold and jewels to rich and poor in Burgundy, and Hagen feared that soon she would win the love of all the people and turn them against him. So, one day, he took the treasure and hid it in the Rhine. He hoped some day to enjoy it himself.

As Hagen now possessed the Nibelung treasure the name "Nibelungs" was given to him and his companions.

5

Etzel, or as we call him, Attila, king of the Huns, heard of the beauty of Kriemhilda and sent one of his knights to ask the queen to become his wife.

At first she refused. However, when she remembered that Etzel carried the sword of Tiew, she changed her mind, because, if she became his wife, she might persuade him to take vengeance upon Gunther and Hagen.

And so it came to pass.

Shortly after their marriage Etzel and Kriemhilda invited Gunther and all his court to a grand midsummer festival in the land of the Huns.

Hagen was afraid to go, for he felt sure that Kriemhilda had not forgiven the murder of Siegfried. However, it was decided that the invitation should be accepted, but that ten thousand knights should go with Gunther as a body-guard.

Shortly after Gunther and his followers arrived at Attila's court a banquet was prepared. Nine thousand Burgundians were seated at the board when Attila's brother came into the banquet hall with a thousand well-armed knights. A quarrel arose and a fight followed.

Thousands of the Burgundians were slain. The struggle continued for days. At last, of all the knights of Burgundy, Gunther and Hagen alone were left alive. Then one of Kriemhilda's friends fought with them and overpowered both. He bound them and delivered them to Kriemhilda.

The queen ordered one of her knights to cut off Gunther's head, and she herself cut off the head of Hagen with "Balmung," Siegfried's wonderful sword. A friend of Hagen then avenged his death by killing Kriemhilda herself.

Of all the Nibelungs who entered the land of the Huns one only ever returned to Burgundy.

Alaric the Visigoth. King from 394-410 A.D.

1

Long before the beginning of the period known as the Middle Ages a tribe of barbarians called the Goths lived north of the River Danube in the country which is now known as Roumania. It was then a part of the great Roman Empire, which at that time had two capitals, Constantinople--the new city of Constantine--and Rome. The Goths had come from the shores of the Baltic Sea and settled on this Roman territory, and the Romans had not driven them back.

During the reign of the Roman Emperor Valens some of the Goths joined a conspiracy against him. Valens punished them for this by crossing the Danube and laying waste their country. At last the Goths had to beg for mercy. The Gothic chief was afraid to set foot on Roman soil, so he and Valens met on their boats in the middle of the Danube and made a treaty of peace.

For a long time the Goths were at war with another tribe of barbarians called Huns. Sometimes the Huns defeated the Goths and drove them to their camps in the mountains. Sometimes the Goths came down to the plains again and defeated the Huns.

At last the Goths grew tired of such constant fighting and thought they would look for new settlements. They sent some of their leading men to the Emperor Valens to ask permission to settle in some country belonging to Rome. The messengers said to the emperor:

"If you will allow us to make homes in the country south of the Danube we will be friends of Rome and fight for her when she needs our help."

The emperor at once granted this request. He said to the Gothic chiefs:

"Rome always needs good soldiers. Your people may cross the Danube and settle on our land. As long as you remain true to Rome we will protect you against your enemies."

These Goths were known as Visigoths, or Western Goths. Other tribes of Goths who had settled in southern Russia, were called Ostrogoths, or Eastern Goths.

After getting permission from the Emperor Valens a large number of the Visigoths crossed the Danube with their families and their cattle and settled in the country now called Bulgaria.

In course of time they became a very powerful nation, and in the year 394 they chose as their king one of the chiefs named Alaric. He was a brave man and a great soldier. Even when a child he took delight in war, and at the age of sixteen he fought as bravely as the older soldiers.

Fig 2. Alaric receiving gifts from the Athenians

One night, not long after he became king, Alaric had a very strange dream. He thought he was driving in a golden chariot through the streets of Rome amid the shouts of the people, who hailed him as emperor. This dream made a deep impression on his mind. He was always thinking of it, and at last he began to have the idea that he could make the dream come true.

"To be master of the Roman Empire," he said to himself, "that is indeed worth trying for; and why should I not try? With my brave soldiers I can conquer Rome, and I shall make the attempt."

So Alaric called his chiefs together and told them what he had made up his mind to do.

The chiefs gave a cry of delight for they approved of the king's proposal. In those days fighting was almost the only business of chiefs, and they were always glad to be at war, especially when there was hope of getting rich spoils. And so the Visigoth chiefs rejoiced at the idea of war against Rome, for they knew that if they were victorious they would have the wealth of the richest city of the world to divide among themselves.

Soon they got ready a great army. With Alaric in command, they marched through Thrace and Macedonia and before long reached Athens. There were now no great warriors in Athens, and the city surrendered to Alaric. The Goths plundered the homes and temples of the Athenians and then marched to the state of Elis, in the southwestern part of Greece. Here a famous Roman general named Stilicho besieged them in their camp. Alaric managed to force his way through the lines of the Romans and escaped. He marched to Epirus. This was a province of Greece that lay on the east side of the Ionian Sea. Arcadius, the Emperor of the East, now made Alaric governor of this district and a large region lying near it. The whole territory was called Eastern Illyricum and formed part of the Eastern Empire.

2

Alaric now set out to make an attack on Rome, the capital of the Western Empire. As soon as Honorius, Emperor of the West, learned that Alaric was approaching, he fled to a strong fortress among the mountains of North Italy. His great general Stilicho came to his rescue and defeated Alaric near Verona. But even after this Honorius was so afraid of Alaric that he made him governor of a part of his empire called Western Illyricum and gave him a large yearly income.

Honorius, however, did not keep certain of his promises to Alaric, who consequently, in the year 408, marched to Rome and besieged it. The cowardly emperor fled to Ravenna, leaving his generals to make terms with Alaric. It was agreed that Alaric should withdraw from Rome upon the payment of 5,000 pounds of gold and 30,000 pounds of silver.

When Honorius read the treaty he refused to sign it. Alaric then demanded that the city be surrendered to him, and the people, terrified, opened their gates and even agreed that Alaric should appoint another emperor in place of Honorius.

This new emperor, however, ruled so badly that Alaric thought it best to restore Honorius. Then Honorius, when just about to be treated so honorably, allowed a barbarian chief who was an ally of his to make an attack upon Alaric. The attack was unsuccessful, and Alaric immediately laid siege to Rome for the third time. The city was taken and Alaric's dream came true. In a grand procession he rode at the head of his army through the streets of the great capital.

Then began the work of destruction. The Goths ran in crowds through the city, wrecked private houses and public buildings and seized everything of value they could find. Alaric gave orders that no injury should be done to the Christian churches, but other splendid buildings of the great city were stripped of the beautiful and costly articles that they contained, and all the gold and silver was carried away from the public treasury.

In the midst of the pillage Alaric dressed himself in splendid robes and sat upon the throne of the emperor, with a golden crown upon his head.

While Alaric was sitting on the throne thousands of Romans were compelled to kneel down on the ground before him and shout out his name as conqueror and emperor. Then the theaters and circuses were opened, and Roman athletes and gladiators had to give performances for the amusement of the conquerors. After six days of pillage and pleasure Alaric and his army marched through the gates, carrying with them the riches of Rome.

Alaric died on his way to Sicily, which he had thought to conquer also. He felt his death coming and ordered his men to bury him in the bed of the river Busento and to put into his grave the richest treasures that he had taken from Rome.

This order was carried out. A large number of Roman slaves were set to work to dig a channel and turn the water of the Busento into it. They made the grave in the bed of the river, put Alaric's body into and closed it up. Then the river was turned back to its old channel. As soon as the grave was covered up, and the water flowed over it, the slaves who had done the work were put to death by the Visigoth chiefs.

Attila the Hun. King from 434-453 A.D.

1

The fierce and warlike tribe, called the Huns, who had driven the Goths to seek new homes, came from Asia into Southeastern Europe and took possession of a large territory lying north of the River Danube.

During the first half of the fifth century the Huns had a famous king named Attila. He was only twenty-one years old when he became their king. But although he was young, he was very brave and ambitious, and he wanted to be a great and powerful king.

Not far from Attila's palace there was a great rocky cave in the mountains. In this cave lived a strange man called the "Hermit of the Rocks." No one knew his real name, or from what country he had come. He was very old, with wrinkled face and long gray hair and beard.

Many persons believed that he was a fortune-teller, so people often went to him to inquire what was to happen to them. One day, shortly after he became king, Attila went to the cave to get his fortune told.

"Wise man," said he, "look into the future and tell me what is before me in the path of life."

The hermit thought for a few moments, and then said, "O King, I see you a famous conqueror, the master of many nations. I see you going from country to country, defeating armies and destroying cities until men call you the 'Fear of the World.' You heap up vast riches, but just after you have married the woman you love grim death strikes you down."

With a cry of horror Attila fled from the cave. For a time he thought of giving up his idea of becoming a great man. But he was young and full of spirit, and very soon he remembered only what had been said to him about his becoming a great and famous conqueror and began to prepare for war. He gathered together the best men from the various tribes of his people and trained them into a great army of good soldiers.

2

About this time one of the king's shepherds, while taking care of cattle in the fields, noticed blood dripping from the foot of one of the oxen. The shepherd followed the streak of blood through the grass and at last found the sharp point of a sword sticking out of the earth. He dug out the weapon, carried it to the palace, and gave it to King Attila. The king declared it was the sword of Tiew, the god of war. He then strapped it to his side and said he would always wear it.

"I shall never be defeated in battle," he cried, "as long as I fight with the sword of Tiew."

As soon as his army was ready he marched with it into countries which belonged to Rome. He defeated the Romans in several great battles and captured many of their cities. The Roman Emperor Theodosius had to ask for terms of peace. Attila agreed that there should be peace, but soon afterwards he found out that Theodosius had formed a plot to murder him. He was so enraged at this that he again began war. He plundered and burned cities wherever he went, and at last the emperor had to give him a large sum of money and a portion of country south of the Danube.

This made peace, but the peace did not last long. In a few years Attila appeared at the head of an army of 700,000 men. With this great force he marched across Germany and into Gaul. He rode on a beautiful black horse, and carried at his side the sword of Tiew. He attacked and destroyed towns and killed the inhabitants without mercy. The people had such dread of him that he was called the "Scourge of God" and the "Fear of the World."

3

Attila and his terrible Huns marched through Gaul until they came to the city of Orleans. Here the people bravely resisted the invaders. They shut their gates and defended themselves in every way they could. In those times all towns of any great size were surrounded by strong walls. There was war constantly going on nearly everywhere, and there were a great many fierce tribes and chiefs who lived by robbing their neighbors. So the towns and castles in which there was much money or other valuable property were not safe without high and strong walls.

Attila tried to take Orleans, but soon after he began to attack the walls he saw a great army at a distance coming towards the city. He quickly gathered his forces together, marched to the neighboring plain of Champagne and halted at the place where the city of Châlons (shah-lon') now stands.

The army which Attila saw was an army of 300,000 Romans and Visigoths. It was led by a Roman general name Aëtius (A-ë'-ti-us) and the Visigoth king Theodoric (The-od'-o-ric). The Visigoths after the death of Alaric had settled in parts of Gaul, and their king had now agreed to join the Romans against the common enemy--the terrible Huns. So the great army of the Romans and Visigoths marched up and attacked the Huns at Châlons. It was a fierce battle. Both sides fought with the greatest bravery. At first the Huns seemed to be winning. They drove back the Romans and Visigoths from the field, and in the fight Theodoric was killed.

Aëtius now began to fear that he would be beaten, but just at that moment Thorismond (Thor'-is-mond), the son of Theodoric, made another charge against the Huns. He had taken command of the Visigoths when his father was killed, and now he led them on to fight. They were all eager to have revenge for the death of their king, so they fought like lions and swept across the plain with great fury. The Huns were soon beaten on every side, and Attila himself fled to his camp. It was the first time he had ever been defeated. Thorismond, the conqueror, was lifted upon his shield on the battle-field and hailed as king of the Visigoths.

When Attila reached his camp he had all his baggage and wagons gathered in a great heap. He intended to set fire to it and jump into the flames if the Romans should come there to attack him.

"Here I will perish in the flames," he cried, "rather than surrender to my enemies."

But the Romans did not come to attack him, and in a few days he marched back to his own country.

Very soon, however, he was again on the war path. This time he invaded Italy. He attacked and plundered the town of Aquileia (Aq'-ui-le'-i-a), and the terrified inhabitants fled for their lives to the hills and mountains. Some of them took refuge in the islands and marshes of the Adriatic Sea. Here they founded Venice.

The people of Rome and the Emperor Valentinian were greatly alarmed at the approach of the dreaded Attila. He was now near the city, and they had no army strong enough to send against him. Rome would have been again destroyed if it had not been for Pope Leo I who went to the camp of Attila and persuaded him not to attack the city. It is said that the barbarian king was awed by the majestic aspect and priestly robes of Leo. It is also told that the apostles Peter and Paul appeared to Attila in his camp and threatened him with death if he should attack Rome. He did not go away, however, without getting a large sum of money as ransom.

4

Shortly after leaving Italy Attila suddenly died. Only the day before his death he had married a beautiful woman whom he loved very much.

The Huns mourned their king in a barbarous way. They shaved their heads and cut themselves on their faces with knives, so that their blood, instead of their tears, flowed for the loss of their great leader. They enclosed his body in three coffins--one of gold, one of silver, and one of iron--and they buried him at night, in a secret spot in the mountains. When the funeral was over, they killed the slaves who had dug the grave, as the Visigoths had done after the burial of Alaric.

After the death of Attila we hear little more of the Huns.

Fig. 3 - Attila meeting Pope Leo the Great, 1360. From a 14th century Hungarian manuscript.

Genseric the Vandal. King from 427-477 A.D.

1

The Vandals were another wild and fierce tribe that came from the shores of the Baltic and invaded central and southern Europe in the later times of the Roman Empire.

In the fifth century some of these people occupied a region in the south of Spain. One of their most celebrated kings was name Genseric (Gen'-ser-ic). He became king in 427, when he was but twenty-one years of age. He was lame in one leg and looked as if he were a very ordinary person.

Like most of the Vandals, he was a cruel and cunning man, but he had great ability in many ways. He fought in battles even when a boy and was known far and wide for his bravery and skill as a leader.

About the time that Genseric became king, the governor of the Roman province in the north of Africa, on the Mediterranean coast, was a man called Count Boniface. This Count Boniface had been a good and loyal officer of Rome; but a plot was formed against him by Aëtius, the general who had fought Attila at Châlons. The Roman emperor at the time of the plot was Valentinian III. He was then too young to act as ruler, so the affairs of government were managed by his mother Placidia (Pla-cid'-i-a).

Aëtius advised Placidia to dismiss Boniface and call him home from Africa. He said the count was a traitor, and that he was going to make war against Rome. At the same time he wrote secretly to Count Boniface and told him that if he came to Rome the empress would put him to death.

Boniface believed this story, and he refused to return to Rome. He also sent a letter to Genseric, inviting him to come to Africa with an army.

Genseric was greatly delighted to receive the invitation from Boniface. He had long wanted to attack Rome and take from her some of the rich countries she had conquered, and now a good opportunity offered. So he got ready a great army of his brave Vandals, and they sailed across the Strait of Gibraltar to Africa.

They soon gained possession of that part of the African coast on which they had landed, and marched into other parts of the coast and captured towns and cities. By this time Boniface had learned all about the wicked plot of Aëtius. He now regretted having invited the Vandals to Africa and tried to induce them to return to Spain, but Genseric sternly refused.

"Never," he said, "shall I go back to Spain until I am master of Africa."

"Then," cried Boniface, "I will drive you back."

Soon afterwards there was a battle between the Romans and Vandals, and the Romans were defeated. They were also defeated in several other battles. At last they had to flee for safety to two or three towns which the Vandals had not yet taken. One of these towns was Hippo.

Genseric captured this town after a siege of thirteen months. Then he burned the churches and other buildings, and laid waste the neighboring country. This was what the Vandals did whenever they took a town, and so the word VANDAL came to mean a person who needlessly or wantonly destroys valuable property.

A great many of the natives of Africa joined the army of Genseric. They had for a long time been ill-treated by the Romans and were glad to see them defeated. Genseric continued his work of conquest until he took the city of Carthage, which he made the capital of his new kingdom in Africa.

But he was not content with conquering merely on land. He built great fleets and sailed over the Mediterranean, capturing trading vessels. For many years he plundered towns along the coasts, so that the name of Genseric became a terror to the people of all the countries bordering the Mediterranean.

2

One day a Roman ship came to Carthage with a messenger from the Empress Eudoxia to Genseric. Eudoxia was the widow of Valentinian III. After ruling several years, Valentinian had just been murdered by a Roman noble named Maximus, who had at once made himself emperor.

When the messenger entered the room where Genseric was, he said:

"Great king, I bring you a message from the Empress Eudoxia. She begs your help. She and her two beautiful daughters are in danger in Rome. She wishes you to protect them against Maximus. She invites you to come with an army to Rome and take the city. She and her friends will help you as much as they can."

With a cry of joy Genseric sprang to his feet and exclaimed:

"Tell the empress that I accept her invitation. I shall set out for Rome immediately. I shall set out for Rome immediately. I shall protect Eudoxia and her friends."

Genseric then got ready a fleet and a great army, and sailed across the Mediterranean to the mouth of the Tiber. When the Emperor Maximus heard that the Vandals were coming he prepared to flee from the city, and he advised the Senate to do the same. The people were so angry at this that they put him to death and threw his body into the river.

Three days later Genseric and his army were at the gates of Rome. There was no one to oppose them, and they marched in and took possession of the city. It was only forty-five years since Alaric had been there and carried off all the valuable things he could find. But since then Rome had become again grand and wealthy, so there was plenty for Genseric and his Vandals to carry away. They spent fourteen days in the work of plunder. They sacked the temples and public buildings and private houses and the emperor's palace, and they took off to their ships immense quantities of gold and silver and jewels and furniture, and destroyed hundreds of beautiful and priceless works of art.

The Vandal king also put to death a number of Roman citizens and carried away many more as slaves. He took Eudoxia and her daughters with him to Carthage. One of the daughters was soon afterwards married to Genseric's eldest son, Hunneric.

3

Some years after the capture of Rome by Genseric, there was a Roman emperor named Majorian (Ma-jo'-ri-an). He was a good ruler and a brave man. The Vandals still continued to attack and plunder cities in Italy and other countries belonging to Rome, and Majorian resolved to punish them. So he got together a great army and built a fleet of three hundred ships to carry his troops to Carthage.

But he first marched his men across the Alps, through Gaul, and down to the seaport of Carthagena in Spain, where his fleet was stationed. He took this route because he expected to add to his forces as he went along. Before sailing with his army for Carthage he wished very much to see with his own eyes what sort of people the Vandals were and whether they were so powerful at home as was generally believed.

So he dyed his hair and disguised himself in other ways and went to Carthage, pretending that he was a messenger or ambassador from the Roman emperor, coming to talk about peace. Genseric received him with respect and entertained him hospitably, not knowing that he was the Emperor Majorian. Of course peace was not made. The emperor left Carthage after having got as much information as he could.

But Genseric did not wait for the Roman fleet to come to attack him in his capital. When he got word that it was in the Bay of Carthagena, he sailed there with a fleet of his own and in a single day burned or sank nearly all the Roman ships.

After this the Vandals became more than ever the terror of the Mediterranean and all the countries bordering upon it. Every year their ships went round the coasts from Asia Minor to Spain, attacking and plundering cities on their way and carrying off prisoners.

All the efforts of the Romans failed to put a stop to these ravages. The Emperor Leo, who ruled over the eastern division of the Empire, fitted out a great fleet at Constantinople to make another attempt to suppress the pirates. There were more than a thousand ships in this fleet and they carried a hundred thousand men. The command of the expedition was given to Basilicus (Bas-il'-i-cus), the brother of Emperor Leo's wife.

Basilicus sailed with his ships to Africa and landed the army not far from Carthage. Genseric asked for a truce for five days to consider terms of peace, and the truce was granted. But the cunning Vandal was not thinking of peace. He only wanted time to carry out a plan he had made to destroy the Roman fleet.

One dark night, during the truce, he filled the largest of his ships with some of the bravest of his soldiers, and they sailed silently and cautiously in among the Roman ships, towing behind them large boats filled with material that would easily burn.

These boats were set on fire and floated against the Roman vessels, which also were soon on fire. The flames quickly spread, and in a very short time a great part of the Roman fleet was destroyed. Basilicus fled with as many ships as he could save, and returned to Constantinople.

This was the last attempt of the Romans to conquer the Vandals. Genseric lived to a good old age, and when he died, in 477, all the countries he had conquered during his life still remained parts of the Vandal dominions.

Theodoric the Ostrogoth. King from 475-526 A.D.

1

The Ostrogoths, or East Goths, who had settled in Southern Russia, at length pushed southward and westward to the mouth of the Danube.

They were continually invading countries belonging to the Romans and their warlike raids were dreaded by the emperors of the Eastern Roman Empire, who lived at Constantinople. One emperor gave them land and money, and thus stopped their invasions for a time.

The most famous of the Ostrogoth kings was Theodoric (The-od'-or-ic) the Great. He was the son of Theodemir (The-od'-e-mir), who was also a king of the Ostrogoths. When Theodoric was eight years old he was sent to Constantinople to be held as a hostage by Leo, the Emperor of the East. In former times, when kings made treaties with one another, it was customary for one to give to the other a pledge or security that he would fulfill the conditions of the treaty. The pledge usually given was some important person or persons, perhaps the king's son or a number of his chief men. Persons so given as a security were called hostages. When Theodoric was a boy he was given as a hostage for his father's good faith in carrying out a treaty with the Emperor and was sent to Constantinople to live. Here the youth was well treated by Leo. He was educated with great care and trained in all the exercises of war.

Theodemir died in 475, and then Theodoric returned to his own country and became king of the Ostrogoths. At this time he was eighteen years of age. He was handsome and brave and people loved him, for in those days a man who was tall and strong and brave was liked by everybody.

2

For some years after he became king Theodoric had frequent wars with other Gothic kings and also with the Roman Emperor Zeno (Ze'-no). He was nearly always successful in battle, and at last Zeno began to think it would be better to try to make friends with him. So he gave Theodoric some rich lands and made him commander of the Imperial Guard of Constantinople.

But the Emperor soon became tired of having the Ostrogoth king at his court, and to get rid of him he agreed that Theodoric should go with his army to Italy, and take that country from Odoacer (O-do-a'-cer). Theodoric was delighted at the proposal and began at once to make his preparations.

Odoacer was at that time king of Italy. Before he became king he had been a general in the army of Romulus Augustulus, the Western Roman Emperor. The soldiers of the army were not satisfied with their pay, and when they asked for more they did not get it. Then they drove Romulus Augustulus from the throne, and chose Odoacer to succeed him. But Odoacer would not take the name of emperor. He was called the "patrician" of Italy, and he ruled the country well.

Theodoric started for Italy, not only with a great army, but with all the people of his country. He meant to take Italy and be its king and settle in it with all his Ostrogoths. When he set out he had with him two hundred and fifty thousand persons--men, women, and children--with a great number of horses and wagons to carry them and their things. He had also an army of sixty thousand brave soldiers.

It was a long and weary journey from the shores of the Black Sea overland to the foot of the Alps Mountains and across the Alps into Italy. Here and there on the way they met savage tribes that tried to stop them, but Theodoric defeated the savages and took a great many of them prisoners. He made these prisoners, women as well as men, help carry the baggage and do other work.

The journey took months, but at last the Ostrogoths reached the top of the Alps. Then they could see, stretched out before them, the beautiful land of Italy. They were all delighted. They shouted and danced with joy, and Theodoric cried out:

"There is the country which shall be our home. Let us march on. It certainly shall be ours."

Then they passed quickly down, and soon they were in Italy. Odoacer had heard of their coming and he got ready an army to drive them away. Theodoric also got his fighting men ready. The two armies met, and there was a great battle near the town of Aquileia. Odoacer was defeated. Then he tried to get Theodoric to leave Italy by offering him a large sum of money.

"I will give you," said he, "thousands of pounds of gold and silver if you agree to go back to your own country."

But Theodoric would not go. He said he had as good a right to be king of Italy as Odoacer, and he would remain and conquer the country and be its king. Soon after there was another battle, near Verona, and Odoacer was again defeated.

Theodoric came very near being killed in battle. He was saved only by the courage of his mother. She was in his camp, and at one time she saw a number of the Ostrogoths running away from that part of the battle-field where her son was fighting, thus leaving him without support. The mother rushed forward and stopped the fleeing men. She made them feel that it was a shame for them to desert their leader, and they at once returned to the field and fought beside their king until the battle was won.

After the battle of Verona, Odoacer went with his army to the city of Ravenna, and remained there for some time. Theodoric followed with his Ostrogoths and tried to take the city, but there was a very strong wall around it, and the Ostrogoths could not capture it. Although Theodoric was not able to take Ravenna, he did not remain idle. He marched off to other parts of the country, and took possession of towns and districts wherever he went.

After a while Odoacer got together a better army than he had before, and made another effort to defeat Theodoric. But he again failed. Theodoric defeated him in another great battle, which was fought on the banks of the River Adda. After this battle Odoacer again fled to Ravenna. Theodoric followed again and laid siege to the city. This time his army surrounded it and kept provisions from being sent in, and at last, when there was no food in the city for the soldiers or the people to eat, Odoacer had to surrender.

A treaty was then made between the two kings and both agreed that they should rule together over Italy, each to have equal power. But a few days afterwards Theodoric murdered Odoacer while sitting at a banquet, and then made himself the sole king of Italy. He divided one-third of the land of the country among his own followers. So the Ostrogoths settled in Italy, and Ostrogoths, Romans, and Visigoths were governed by Theodoric as one people.

Theodoric died at the age of seventy-one after ruling Italy for thirty-three years.

Clovis. King from 481-511 A.D.

1

While the power of the Roman Empire was declining there dwelt on the banks of the River Rhine a number of savage Teuton tribes called Franks. The word Frank means FREE, and those tribes took pride in being known as Franks or freemen.

The Franks occupied the east bank of the Rhine for about two hundred years. Then many of the tribes crossed the river in search of new homes. The region west of the river was at that time called Gaul. Here the Franks established themselves and became a powerful people. From their name the country was afterwards called FRANCE.

Each tribe of the Franks had its own king. The greatest of all these kings was Chlodwig, or Clovis, as we call him, who became ruler of his tribe in the year 481, just six years after Theodoric became king of the Ostrogoths. Clovis was then only sixteen years of age. But though he was so young he proved in a very short time that he could govern as well as older men. He was intelligent and brave. No one ever knew him to be afraid of anything even when he was but a child. His father, who was named Childeric (chil'-der-ic), often took him to wars which the Franks had with neighboring tribes, and he was very proud of his son's bravery. The young man was also a bold and skillful horseman. He could tame and ride the most fiery horse.

When Clovis became king of the Franks a great part of Gaul still belonged to Rome. This part was then governed by a Roman general, named Syagrius (sy-ag'-ri-us). Clovis resolved to drive the Romans out of the country, and he talked over the matter with the head men of his army.

"My desire," said he, "is that the Franks shall have possession of every part of this fair land. I shall drive the Romans and their friends away and make Gaul the empire of the Franks."

2

At this time the Romans had a great army in Gaul. It was encamped near the city of Soissons (swah-son') and was commanded by Syagrius. Clovis resolved to attack it and led his army at once to Soissons. When he came near the city he summoned Syagrius to surrender. Syagrius refused and asked for an interview with the commander of the Franks. Clovis consented to meet him, and an arrangement was made that the meeting should take place in the open space between the two armies. When Clovis stepped out in front of his own army, accompanied by some of his savage warriors, Syagrius also came forward. But the moment he saw the king of the Franks he laughed loudly and exclaimed:

"A boy! A boy has come to fight me! The Franks with a boy to lead them have come to fight the Romans."

Clovis was very angry at this insulting language and shouted back:

"Ay, but this boy will conquer you."

Fig 4. French Coin - "Clovis, King of France"

Then both sides prepared for battle. The Romans thought that they would win the victory easily, but they were mistaken. Every time that they made a charge upon the Franks they were beaten back by the warriors of Clovis. The young king himself fought bravely at the head of his men and with his own sword struck down a number of the Romans. He tried to find Syagrius and fight with him; but the Roman commander was nowhere to be found. Early in the battle he had fled from the field, leaving his men to defend themselves as best they could.

The Franks gained a great victory. With their gallant boy king leading them on they drove the Roman's before them, and when the battle was over they took possession of the city of Soissons. Clovis afterwards conquered all the other Frankish chiefs and made himself king of all the Franks.

3

Not very long after Clovis became king he heard of a beautiful young girl, the niece of Gondebaud (gon'-de-baud), king of Burgundy, and he thought he would like to marry her. Her name was Clotilde (clo-tilde'), and she was an orphan, for her wicked uncle Gondebaud had killed her father and mother. Clovis sent one of his nobles to Gondebaud to ask her for his wife. At first Gondebaud thought of refusing to let the girl go. He feared that she might have him punished for the murder of her parents if she became the wife of so powerful a man as Clovis. But he was also afraid that by refusing he would provoke the anger of Clovis; so he permitted the girl to be taken to the court of the king of the Franks. Clovis was delighted when he saw her; and they were immediately married.

Clotilde was a devout Christian, and she wished very much to convert her husband, who, like most of his people, was a worshiper of the heathen gods. But Clovis was not willing to give up his own religion. Nevertheless Clotilde continued to do every thing she could to persuade him to become a Christian.

Soon after his marriage Clovis had a war with a tribe called the Alemanni. This tribe had crossed the Rhine from Germany and taken possession of some of the eastern provinces of Gaul. Clovis speedily got his warriors together and marched against them. A battle was fought at a place called Tolbiac, not far from the present city of Cologne. In this battle the Franks were nearly beaten, for the Alemanni were fierce and brave men and skillful fighters. When Clovis saw his soldiers driven back several times he began to lose hope, but at that moment he thought of his pious wife and of the powerful God of whom she had so often spoken. Then he raised his hands to heaven and earnestly prayed to that God.

"O God of Clotilde," he cried, "help me in this my hour of need. If thou wilt give me victory now I will believe in thee."

Almost immediately the course of the battle began to change in favor of the Franks. Clovis led his warriors forward once more, and this time the Alemanni fled before them in terror. The Franks gained a great victory, and they believed it was in answer to the prayer of their king.

When Clovis returned home he did not forget his promise. He told Clotilde how he had prayed to her God for help and how his prayer had been heard, and he said he was now ready to become a Christian. Clotilde was very happy on hearing this, and she arranged that her husband should be baptized in the church of Rheims on the following Christmas day.

Meanwhile Clovis issued a proclamation to his people declaring that he was a believer in Christ, and giving orders that all the images and temples of the heathen gods should be destroyed. This was immediately done, and many of the people followed his example and became Christians.

Clovis was a very earnest and fervent convert. One day the bishop of Rheims, while instructing him in the doctrines of Christianity, described the death of Christ. As the bishop proceeded Clovis became much excited, and at last jumped up from his seat and exclaimed:

"Had I been there with my brave Franks I would have avenged His wrongs."

On Christmas day a great multitude assembled in the church at Rheims to witness the baptism of the king. A large number of his fierce warriors were baptized at the same time. The service was performed with great ceremony by the bishop of Rheims, and the title of "Most Christian King" was conferred on Clovis by the Pope. This title was ever afterwards borne by the kings of France.

Like most of the kings and chiefs of those rude and barbarous times, Clovis often did cruel and wicked things. When Rheims was captured, before he became a Christian, a golden vase was taken by some soldiers from the church. The bishop asked Clovis to have it returned, and Clovis bade him wait until the division of spoils. All the valuable things taken by soldiers in war were divided among the whole army, each man getting his share according to rank. Such things were called spoils.

When the next time came for dividing spoils Clovis asked that he might have the vase over and above his regular share, his intention being to return it to the bishop. But one of the soldiers objected, saying that the king should have no more than his fair share, and at the same time shattered the vase with his ax. Clovis was very angry, but at the time said nothing. Soon afterwards, however, there was the usual examination of the arms of the soldiers to see that they were in proper condition for active service. Clovis himself took part in the examination, and when he came to the soldier who had broken the vase he found fault with the condition of his weapons and with one blow of his battle-ax struck the man dead.

4

The next war that Clovis engaged in was with some tribes of the Goths who occupied the country called Aquitaine lying south of the River Loire. He defeated them and added Aquitaine to the kingdom of the Franks.

Clovis afterwards made war upon other people of Gaul and defeated them. At last all the provinces from the lower Rhine to the Pyrenees Mountains were compelled to acknowledge him as king. He then went to reside at the city of Paris, which he made the capital of his kingdom. He died there A.D. 511.

The dynasty or family of kings to which he belonged is known in history as the Merovingian dynasty. It was so called from Merovæus (Me-ro-væ'-us), the father of Childeric and grandfather of Clovis.

Justinian the Great. Emperor from 527-565 A.D.

1

In the time of Clovis the country now called Bulgaria was inhabited by Goths. One day a poor shepherd boy, about sixteen years of age, left his mountain home in that country to go to the city of Constantinople, which was many miles away. The boy had no money to pay the expenses of the journey, but he was determined to go, even though he should have to walk every step of the road and live on fruits that he could gather by the way. He was a bright, clever boy who had spent his life hitherto in a village, but was now eager to go out into the world to seek his fortune.

Some years before, this boy's uncle, who was named Justin, had gone to Constantinople and joined the Roman army. He was so brave and so good a soldier that he soon came to be commander of the imperial guard which attended the emperor.

The poor shepherd boy had heard of the success of his uncle, and this was the reason why he resolved to set off for the big city. So he started down the mountain and trudged along the valley in high hope, feeling certain that he would reach the end of his journey in safety. It was a difficult and dangerous journey, and it took him several weeks, for he had to go through dark forests and to cross rivers and high hills; but at last one afternoon in midsummer he walked through the main gate of Constantinople, proud and happy that he had accomplished his purpose.

He had no trouble in finding his Uncle Justin; for everybody in Constantinople knew the commander of the emperor's guards. And when the boy appeared at the great man's house and told who he was, his uncle received him with much kindness. He took him into his own family, and gave him the best education that could be had in the city.

As the boy was very talented and eager for knowledge he soon became an excellent scholar. He grew up a tall, good-looking man, with black eyes and curly hair, and he was always richly dressed. He was well liked at the emperor's court, and was respected by everybody on account of his learning.

2

One day a great change came for both uncle and nephew. The emperor died; and the people chose Justin to succeed him. He took the title of Justinus I (Jus-ti'-nus), and so the young scholar, who had once been a poor shepherd boy, was now nephew of an emperor.

After some years Justinus was advised by his nobles to take the young man, who had adopted the name of Justinian, to help him in ruling the empire. Justinus agreed to this proposal, for he was now old and in feeble health, and not able himself to attend to the important affairs of government. He therefore called the great lords of his court together and in their presence he placed a crown on the head of his nephew, who thus became joint emperor with his uncle. The uncle died only a few months after, and then Justinian was declared emperor. This was in the year 527. Justinian reigned for nearly forty years and did so many important things that he was afterwards called Justinian the Great.

He had many wars during his reign, but he himself did not take part in them. He was not experienced as a soldier, for he had spent most of his time in study. He was fortunate enough, however, to have two great generals to lead his armies. One of them was named Belisarius and the other Narses.

Belisarius was one of the greatest soldiers that ever lived. He gained wonderful victories for Justinian, and conquered some of the old Roman provinces that had been lost for many years.

The victories of these two generals largely helped to make the reign of Justinian remarkable in history. Many years before he ascended the throne the Vandals, as you have read, conquered the northern part of Africa and established a kingdom there with Carthage as its capital. The Vandal king in the time of Justinian was named Gelimer (Gel'-i-mer), and he lived in Carthage.

Justinian resolved to make war on this king in order to recover Northern Africa and make it again a part of the Empire. So Belisarius was sent to Africa with an army of thirty-five thousand men and five thousand horses, that were carried on a fleet of six hundred ships. It took this fleet three months to make the voyage from Constantinople to Africa. The same voyage may now be made in a very few days. But in the time of Belisarius there were no steamships, and nothing was known of the power of steam for moving machinery. The ships or galleys were sailing vessels; and when there was no wind they could make no progress except by rowing.

When Belisarius reached Africa he left five men as a guard in each vessel, and with the body of his army he marched for some days along the coast. The people received him in a friendly way, for they had grown tired of the rule of the Vandals, and preferred to be under the government of the Romans.

About ten miles from Carthage he met a large army led by the brother of Gelimer. A battle immediately took place, and the Vandals were utterly defeated. Gelimer's brother was killed, and the king himself, who had followed with another army and joined the fight, was also defeated and fled from the field. Belisarius then proceeded to Carthage and took possession of the city.

Soon afterwards Gelimer collected another army and fought the Romans in another battle, twenty miles from Carthage; but Belisarius again defeated him and the Vandal king again fled. This was the end of the Vandal king in Africa. In a short time Gelimer gave himself up to Belisarius, who took him to Constantinople. Justinian set apart an estate for him to live upon, and the conquered king passed the rest of his life in peaceful retirement.

After conquering the Vandals Justinian resolved to conquer Italy, which was then held by the Ostrogoths. A large army was got together and put under the command of Belisarius and Narses, who immediately set out for Italy. When they arrived there they marched straight to Rome, and after some fighting took possession of the city. But in a few months, Vitiges (vit'-i-ges), king of the Goths, appeared with an army before the gates and challenged Belisarius and Narses to come out and fight.

The Roman generals, however, were not then ready to fight, and so the Ostrogoth king laid siege to the city, thinking that he would compel the Romans to surrender.

But instead of having any thought of surrender, Belisarius was preparing his men for fight, and when they were ready he attacked Vitiges and defeated him. Vitiges retired to Ravenna, and Belisarius quickly followed, and made such an assault on the city that it was compelled to surrender. The Ostrogoth army was captured, and Vitiges was taken to Constantinople a prisoner.

Belisarius and Narses then went to Northern Italy, and, after a long war, conquered all the tribes there. Thus the power of Justinian was established throughout the whole country, and the city of Rome was again under the dominion of a Roman emperor.

While his brave generals were winning these victories for the Empire, Justinian himself was busy in making improvements of various kinds at the capital. He erected great public buildings, which were not only useful but ornamental to the city. The most remarkable of them was the very magnificent cathedral of St. Sophia (So-phi'-a), for a long time the grandest church structure in the world. The great temple still exists in all its beauty and grandeur, but is now used as a Mohammedan mosque.

But the most important thing that Justinian did--the work for which he is most celebrated--was the improving and collecting of the laws. He made many excellent new laws and reformed many of the old laws, so that he became famous as one of the greatest of the world's legislators. For a long time the Roman laws had been difficult to understand. There was a vast number of them, and different writers differed widely as to what the laws really were and what they meant. Justinian employed a great lawyer, named Tribonian (trib-o'-ni-an), to collect and simplify the principal laws. The collection which he made was called the CODE OF JUSTINIAN. It still exists, and is the model according to which most of the countries of Europe have made their laws.

Justinian also did a great deal of good by establishing a number of manufactures in Constantinople. It was he who first brought silk-worms into Europe.

To the last year of his life Justinian was strong and active and a hard worker. He often worked or studied all day and all night without eating or sleeping. He died in 565 at the age of eighty-three years.

Fig. 5. Coin commemorating Justinian's conquests of Africa, c. 535

Fig. 6 - Mosaik in Ravenna, Italy, showing the Court of Emperor Justinian (Basilica di San Vitale)

Mohammed. Lived from 570-632 A.D.

1

A great number of people in Asia and Africa and much of those in Turkey in Europe profess the Mohammedan (Mo-ham'-me-dan) religion. They are called Mohammedans, Mussulmans (Mus'-sul-mans) or Moslems; and the proper name for their religion is "Islam," which means obedience, or submission.

The founder of this religion was a man named Mohammed (Mo-ham'-med), or Mahomet (Ma-hom'-et). He was born in the year 570, in Mecca, a city of Arabia. His parents were poor people, though, it is said, they were descended from Arabian princes. They died when Mohammed was a child, and his uncle, a kind-hearted man named AbuTalib (A'-bu-Ta-lïb'), took him home and brought him up.

When the boy grew old enough he took care of his uncle's sheep and camels. Sometimes he went on journeys with his uncle to different parts of Arabia, to help him in his business as a trader. On these journeys Mohammed used to ride on a camel, and he soon became a skillful camel-driver.

Mohammed was very faithful and honest in all his work. He always spoke the truth and never broke a promise. "I have given my promise," he would say, "and I must keep it." He became so well known in Mecca for being truthful and trustworthy that people gave him the name of El Amin, which means "the truthful."

At this time he was only sixteen years of age; but the rich traders had so much confidence in him that they gave him important business to attend to, and trusted him with large sums of money. He often went with caravans to a port on the shore of the Red Sea, sixty-five miles from Mecca, and sold there the goods carried by the camels. Then he guided the long line of camels back to Mecca, and faithfully paid over to the owners of the goods the money he had received.

Mohammed had no school education. He could neither read nor write. But he was not ignorant. He knew well how to do the work intrusted to him, and was a first-rate man of business.

2

One day, when Mohammed was about twenty-five years old, he was walking through the bazaar or market-place, of Mecca when he met the chief camel-driver of a wealthy woman named Khadijah (Kha-dï'-jah). This woman was a widow, who was carrying on the business left her by her husband. As soon as the camel-driver saw Mohammed he stopped him and said:

"My mistress wishes to see you before noon. I think she intends to engage you to take charge of her caravans."

Mohammed waited to hear no more. As quickly as possible he went to the house of Khadijah; for he was well pleased at the thought of being employed in so important a service. The widow received him in a very friendly way. She said:

"I have heard much of you among the traders. They say that though you are so young you are a good caravan manager and can be trusted. Are you willing to take charge of my caravans and give your whole time and service to me?"

Mohammed was delighted.

"I accept your offer," said he, "and I shall do all I can to serve and please you."

Khadijah then engaged him as the manager of her business; and he served her well and faithfully. She thought a great deal of him, and he was much attracted to her, and soon they came to love one another and were married.

As he was now the husband of a rich woman he did not need to work very hard. He still continued to attend to his wife's business; but he did not make so many journeys as before. He spent much of his time in thinking about religion. He learned all that he could about Judaism and Christianity; but he was not satisfied with either of them.

At that time most of the people of Arabia worshiped idols. Very few of them were Christians.

Mohammed was very earnest and serious. In a cave on Mount Hira, near Mecca, he spent several weeks every year in prayer and religious meditation. He declared that, while praying in his cave, he often had visions of God and heaven. He said that many times the angel Gabriel appeared to him and revealed to him the religion which he afterwards taught his followers. As he himself could not write, he committed to memory all that the angel told him, and had it written in a book. This book is called the "Koran," which means, like our own word Bible, the "Book." The Koran is the Bible of Mohammedans.

3

When Mohammed returned home after the angel had first spoken to him, he told his wife of what he had seen and heard. She at once believed and so became a convert to the new religion. She fell upon her knees at the feet of her husband and cried out:

"There is but one God. Mohammed is God's prophet."

Mohammed then told the story to other members of his family. Some of them believed and became his first followers. Soon afterwards he began to preach to the people. He spoke in the market and other public places. Most of those who heard him laughed at what he told them; but some poor people and a few slaves believed him and adopted the new religion. Others said he was a dreamer and a fool.

Fig. 7 – Mohammed teaching his followers

Mohammed, however, paid no heed to the insults he received. He went on telling about the appearance of Gabriel and preaching the doctrines which he said the angel had ordered him to teach the people.

Often while speaking in public Mohammed had what he called a "vision of heavenly things." At such times his face grew pale as death, his eyes became red and staring, he spoke in a loud voice, and his body trembled violently. Then he would tell what he had seen in his vision.

After a time the number of his followers began to increase. People came from distant parts of Arabia and from neighboring countries to hear him. One day six of the chief men of Medina (Me-dï'-na), one of the largest cities of Arabia, listened earnestly to his preaching and were converted. When they returned home they talked of the new religion to their fellow-citizens, and a great many of them became believers.

But the people of Mecca, Mohammed's own home, were nearly all opposed to him. They would not believe what he preached, and they called him an impostor. The people of the tribe to which he himself belonged were the most bitter against him. They even threatened to put him to death as an enemy of the gods.

About this time Mohammed's uncle and wife died, and he had then hardly any friends in Mecca. He therefore resolved to leave that city and go to Medina. Numbers of the people there believed his doctrines and wished him to come and live among them. So he secretly left his native town and fled from his enemies. With a few faithful companions he made his escape to Medina.

It was in the year of our Lord 622 that Mohammed fled from Mecca. This event is very important in Mohammedan history. It is called "the flight of the prophet," or "the Hejira (Hej'-i-ra)," a word which means FLIGHT. The Hejira is the beginning of the Mohammedan era; and so in all countries where the rulers and people are Mohammedans, the years are counted from the Hejira instead of from the birth of Christ.

On his arrival in Medina the people received Mohammed with great rejoicing. He lived there the remainder of his life. A splendid church was built for him in Medina. It was called a mosque, and all Mohammedan churches, or places of worship, are called by this name. It means a place for prostration or prayer.

4

Mohammed thought that it was right to spread his religion by force, and to make war on "unbelievers", as he called all people who did not accept his teaching. He therefore got together an army and fought battles and unbelievers. He gained many victories. He marched against Mecca with an army of ten thousand men, and the city surrendered with little resistance. The people then joined his religion and destroyed their idols. Before very long all the inhabitants of Arabia and many of the people of the neighboring countries became Mohammedans.

Mohammed died in Medina in the year of our Lord 632, or year 11 of the Hejira. He was buried in the mosque in which he had held religious services for so many years; and Medina has ever since been honored, because it contains the tomb of the Prophet. It is believed by his followers that the body still lies in the coffin in the same state as when it was first buried. There is also a story that the coffin of Mohammed rests somewhere between heaven and earth, suspended in the air. But this fable was invented by enemies to bring ridicule on the prophet and his religion.

The tomb of Mohammed is visited every year by people from all Mohammedan countries. Mecca, the birthplace of the prophet, is also visited by vast numbers of pilgrims. Every Mussulman is bound by his religion to make a visit or pilgrimage to Mecca at least once in his life. Whenever a Mussulman prays, no matter in what part of the world he may be, he turns his face towards Mecca, as if he were always thinking of going there.

Good Mohammedans pray five times every day, and there is a church officer called a muezzin (mu-ez'-zin), who gives them notice of the hour for prayer. This he does by going on the platform, or balcony, of the minaret, or tower, of the mosque and chanting in a loud voice such words as these:

"Come to prayer, come to prayer. There is no god but God. He giveth life, and he dieth not. I praise his perfection. God is great."

In Mecca there is a mosque called the Great Mosque. It is a large enclosure in the form of a quadrangle, or square, which can hold 35,000 persons. It is enclosed by arcades with pillars of marble and granite, and has nineteen gates, each with a minaret or pointed tower above it.

Within this enclosure is a famous building called the "Kaaba (Ka'-a-ba)," or cube. It is nearly a cube in shape. It its wall, at one corner, is the celebrated "Black Stone." Moslems regard this stone with the greatest reverence. They say that it came down from heaven. It is said to have been once white, but has become dark from being wept upon and touched by so many millions of pilgrims. It really is reddish-brown in color.

Before the time of Mohammed the Kaaba was a pagan temple; but when he took possession of Mecca he made the old temple the centre of worship for his own religion.

After Mohammed died a person was appointed to be his successor as head of the Moslem church. He was called the caliph, a word which means SUCCESSOR; and this title has been borne ever since by the religious chief of the Mohammedans. In modern times the sultans or rulers of Turkey have been commonly regarded as the caliphs. Arab scholars, however, say that really the sherif (she-rïf'), i.e., the governor of Mecca, is entitled by the Koran to hold this position.

Charles Martel, 714-741 A.D. and Pepin, 741-768 A.D.

1

After the death of Mohammed the Saracens, as Mohammedans are also called, became great warriors. They conquered many countries and established the Mohammedan religion in them. In 711 the Saracens invaded and conquered a great part of Spain and founded a powerful kingdom there, which lasted about seven hundred years.

They intended to conquer the land of the Franks next, and then all Europe.

They thought it would be easy to conquer the Franks, because the Frankish king at that time was a very weak man. He was one of a number of kings who were called the "Do-nothings." They reigned from about 638 to 751. They spent all their time in amusements and pleasures, leaving the affairs of the government to be managed by persons called MAYORS OF THE PALACE.

The mayors of the palace were officers who at first managed the king's household. Afterwards they were made guardians of kings who came to the throne when very young. So long as the king was under age the mayor of the palace acted as chief officer of the government in his name. And as several of the young kings, even when they were old enough to rule, gave less attention to business than to pleasure, the mayors continued to do all the business, until at last they did everything that the king ought to have done. They made war, led armies in battle, raised money and spent it, and carried on the government as they pleased, without consulting the king.

The "Do-nothings" had the title of king, but nothing more. In fact, they did not desire to have any business to do. The things they cared for were dogs, horses and sport.

One of the most famous of the mayors was a man named Pepin (Pep'-in). Once a year, it is said, Pepin had the king dressed in his finest clothes and paraded through the city of Paris, where the court was held. A splendid throng of nobles and courtiers accompanied the king, and did him honor as he went along the streets in a gilded chariot drawn by a long line of beautiful horses. The king was cheered by the people, and he acknowledged their greetings most graciously.

After the parade the king was escorted to the great hall of the palace, which was filled with nobles. Seated on a magnificent throne, he saluted the assemblage and made a short speech. The speech was prepared beforehand by Pepin, and committed to memory by the king. At the close of the ceremony the royal "nobody" retired to his country house and was not heard of again for a year.

Pepin died in 714 A.D., and his son Charles, who was twenty-five years old at that time, succeeded him as mayor of the palace. This Charles is known in history as Charles Martel. He was a brave young man. He had fought in many of his father's battles and so had become a skilled soldier. His men were devoted to him.

While he was mayor of the palace he led armies in several wars against the enemies of the Franks. The most important of his wars was one with the Saracens, who came across the Pyrenees from Spain and invaded the land of the Franks, intending to establish Mohammedanism there. Their army was led by Abd-er-Rahman (Abd-er-Rah'-man), the Saracen governor of Spain.

On his march through the southern districts of the land of the Franks Abd-er-Rahman destroyed many towns and villages, killed a number of the people, and seized all the property he could carry off. He plundered the city of Bordeaux (bor-do'), and, it is said, obtained so many valuable things that every soldier "was loaded with golden vases and cups and emeralds and other precious stones."

But meanwhile Charles Martel was not idle. As quickly as he could he got together a great army of Franks and Germans and marched against the Saracens. The two armies met between the cities of Tours and Poitiers (pwaw-te-ay) in October, 732. For six days there was nothing but an occasional skirmish between small parties from both sides; but on the seventh day a great battle took place.

Both Christians and Mohammedans fought with terrible earnestness. The fight went on all day, and the field was covered with the bodies of the slain. But towards evening, during a resolute charge made by the Franks, Abd-er-Rahman was killed. Then the Saracens gradually retired to their camp.

It was not yet known, however, which side had won; and the Franks expected that the fight would be renewed in the morning.

But when Charles Martel, with his Christian warriors, appeared on the field at sunrise there was no enemy to fight. The Mohammedans had fled in the silence and darkness of the night and had left behind them all their valuable spoils. There was now no doubt which side had won.

The battle of Tours, or Poitiers, as it should be called, is regarded as one of the decisive battles of the world. It decided that Christians, and not Moslems, should be the ruling power in Europe.

Charles Martel is especially celebrated as the hero of this battle. It is said that the name MARTEL was given to him because of his bravery during the fight. Marteau (mar-to') is the French word for hammer, and one of the old French historians says that as a hammer breaks and crushes iron and steel, so Charles broke and crushed the power of his enemies in the battle of Tours.

But though the Saracens fled from the battlefield of Tours, they did not leave the land of the Franks; and Charles had to fight other battles with them, before they were finally defeated. At last, however, he drove them across the Pyrenees, and they never again attempted to invade Frankland.

After his defeat of the Saracens Charles Martel was looked upon as the great champion of Christianity; and to the day of his death, in 741, he was in reality, though not in name, the king of the Franks.

3

Charles Martel had two sons, Pepin and Carloman. For a time they ruled together, but Carloman wished to lead a religious life, so he went to a monastery and became a monk. Then Pepin was sole ruler.

Pepin was quite low in stature, and therefore was called Pepin the Short. But he had great strength and courage. A story is told of him, which shows how fearless he was.

One day he went with a few of his nobles to a circus to see a fight between a lion and a bull. Soon after the fight began, it looked as though the bull was getting the worst of it. Pepin cried out to his companions:

"Will one of you separate the beasts?"

But there was no answer. None of them had the courage to make the attempt. Then Pepin jumped from his seat, rushed into the arena, and with a thrust of his sword killed the lion.

In the early years of Pepin's rule as mayor of the palace the throne was occupied by a king named Childeric (Chil'-der-ic) III. Like his father and the other "do-nothing" kings, Childeric cared more for pleasures and amusements than for affairs of government. Pepin was the real ruler, and after a while he began to think that he ought to have the title of king, as he had all the power and did all the work of governing and defending the kingdom.

So he sent some friends to Rome to consult the Pope. They said to His Holiness:

"Holy father, who ought to be the king of France--the man who has the title, or the man who has the power and does all the duties of king?"

"Certainly," replied the Pope, "the man who has the power and does the duties."

"Then, surely," said they, "Pepin ought to be the king of the Franks; for he has all the power."

The Pope gave his consent, and Pepin was crowned king of the Franks; and thus the reign of Childeric ended and that of Pepin began.

During nearly his whole reign Pepin was engaged in war. Several times he went to Italy to defend the Pope against the Lombards. These people occupied certain parts of Italy, including the province still called Lombardy.

Pepin conquered them and gave as a present to the Pope that part of their possessions which extended for some distance around Rome. This was called "Pepin's Donation." It was the beginning of what is known as the "temporal power" of the Popes, that is, their power as rulers of part of Italy.

Pepin died in 768.

Charlemagne. King from 768-814 A.D.

1

Pepin had two sons Charles and Carloman. After the death of their father they ruled together, but in a few years Carloman died, and then Charles became sole king.

This Charles was the most famous of the kings of the Franks. He did so many great and wonderful things that he is called Charlemagne (shar-le-main'), which means Charles the Great.

He was a great soldier. For thirty years he carried on a war against the Saxons. Finally he conquered them, and their great chief, Wittekind, submitted to him. The Saxons were a people of Germany, who then lived near the land of the Franks. They spoke the same language and were of the same race as the Franks, but had not been civilized by contact with the Romans.

They were still pagans, just as the Franks had been before Clovis became a Christian. They actually offered human sacrifices.

After Charlemagne conquered them he made their lands part of his kingdom. A great number of them, among whom was Wittekind, then became Christians and were baptized; and soon they had churches and schools in many parts of their country.

Another of Charlemagne's wars was against the Lombards.

Pepin, as you have read, had defeated the Lombards and given to the Pope part of the country held by them. The Lombard king now invaded the Pope's lands and threatened Rome itself; so the Pope sent to Charlemagne for help.

Charlemagne quickly marched across the Alps and attacked the Lombards. He drove them out of the Pope's lands and took possession of their country.

After he had conquered the Lombards he carried on war, in 778, in Spain. A large portion of Spain was then held by the Moorish Saracens. But a Mohammedan leader from Damascus had invaded their country, and the Moors invited Charlemagne to help them. He therefore led an army across the Pyrenees. He succeeded in putting his Moorish friends in possession of their lands in Spain and then set out on his return to his own country.

On the march his army was divided into two parts. The main body was led by Charlemagne himself. The rear guard was commanded by a famous warrior named Roland. While marching through the narrow pass of Roncesvalles (ron-thes-val'-yes), among the Pyrenees, Roland's division was attacked by a tribe called the Basques (basks), who lived on the mountain slopes of the neighboring region.

High cliffs walled in the pass on either side. From the tops of these cliffs the Basques hurled down rocks and trunks of trees upon the Franks, and crushed many of them to death. Besides this, the wild mountaineers descended into the pass and attacked them with weapons. Roland fought bravely; but at last he was overpowered, and he and all his men were killed.

Roland had a friend and companion named Oliver, who was as brave as himself. Many stories and songs have been written telling of the wonderful adventures they were said to have had and of their wonderful deeds in war.

The work of Charlemagne in Spain was quickly undone; for Abd-er-Rahman, the leader of the Mohammedans who had come from Damascus, soon conquered almost all the territory south of the Pyrenees.

For more than forty years Charlemagne was king of the Franks; but a still greater dignity was to come to him. In the year 800 some of the people in Rome rebelled against the Pope, and Charlemagne went with an army to put down the rebellion. He entered the city with great pomp and soon conquered the rebels. On Christmas day he went to the church of St. Peter, and as he knelt before the altar the Pope placed a crown upon his head, saying:

"Long live Charles Augustus, Emperor of the Romans."

The people assembled in the church shouted the same words; and so Charlemagne was now emperor of the Western Roman Empire, as well as king of the Franks [the emperors of Constantinople still called themselves Roman Emperors, and still claimed Italy, Germany and France as parts of their empire, though really their authority had not been respected in these countries for more than 300 years.].

Charlemagne built a splendid palace at Aix-la-Chapelle (aks-la-shap-el'), a town in Germany, where perhaps he was born.

Charlemagne was a tall man, with long, flowing beard, and of noble appearance. He dressed in very simple style; but when he went into battle he wore armor, as was the custom for kings and nobles, and often for ordinary soldiers in his day.

Armor was made of leather or iron, or both together. There was a helmet of iron for the head, and a breastplate to cover the breast, or a coat of mail to cover the body. The coat of mail was made of small iron or steel rings linked together, or fastened on to a leather shirt. Coverings for the legs and feet were often attached to the coat.

2

Charlemagne was a great king in may other ways besides the fighting of battles. He did much for the good of his people. He made many excellent laws and appointed judges to see that the laws were carried out. He established schools and placed good teachers in charge of them. He had a school in his palace for his own children, and he employed as their teacher a very learned Englishman named Alcuin (al'-kwin).

In those times few people could read or write. There were not many schools anywhere, and in most places there were none at all. Even the kings had little education. Indeed, few of them could write their own names, and most of them did not care about sending their children to school. They did not think that reading or writing was of much use; but thought that it was far better for boys to learn to be good soldiers, and for girls to learn to spin and weave.

Charlemagne had a very different opinion. He was fond of learning; and whenever he heard of a learned man, living in any foreign country, he tried to get him to come and live in Frankland.

The fame of Charlemagne as a great warrior and a wise emperor spread all over the world. Many kings sent messengers to him to ask his friendship, and bring him presents. Harun-al-Rashid (hah-roon'-al-rash'-eed), the famous caliph, who lived at Bagdad, in Asia, sent him an elephant and a clock which struck the hours.

The Franks were much astonished at the sight of the elephant; for they had never seen one before. They also wondered much at the clock. In those days there were in Europe no clocks such as we have; but water-clocks and hour-glasses were used in some places. The water-clock was a vessel into which water was allowed to trickle. It contained a float which pointed to a scale of hours at the side of the vessel. The float gradually rose as the water trickled in.

The hour-glasses measured time by the falling of fine sand from the top to the bottom of a glass vessel made with a narrow neck in the middle for the sand to go through. They were like the little glasses called egg-timers, which are used for measuring the time for boiling eggs.

Charlemagne died in 814. He was buried in the church which he had built at Aix-la-Chapelle. His body was placed in the tomb, seated upon a grand chair, dressed in royal robes, with a crown on the head, a sword at the side, and a Bible in the hands.

This famous emperor is known in history as Charlemagne, which is the French word for the German name Karl der Grosse (Charles the Great), the name by which he was called at his own court during his life. The German name would really be a better name for him; for he was a German, and German was the language that he spoke. The common name of his favorite residence, Aix-la-Chapelle, also is French, but he knew the place as Aachen (ä'-chen).

The great empire which Charlemagne built up held together only during the life of his son. Then it was divided among his three grandsons. Louis took the eastern part, Lothaire (Lo-thaire') took the central part, with the title of emperor, and Charles took the western part.

Fig. 8 – Charlemagne and Pope Adrian I. In 772, when Pope Adrian I was threatened by invaders, Charlemagne went to Rome to help.

Harun-al-Rashid. Caliph from 786-809 A.D.

1

The most celebrated of all Mohammedan caliphs was Harun-al-Rashid, which means, in English, Aaron the Just. Harun is the hero of several of the stories of the "Arabian Nights," a famous book, which perhaps you have read. There are many curious and wonderful tales in it.

When Harun was only eighteen years old he showed such courage and skill as a soldier that his father, who was then caliph, allowed him to lead an army against the enemies of the Mohammedans; and he won many great victories.

He afterwards commanded an army of ninety-five thousand Arabs and Persians, sent by his father to invade the Eastern Roman Empire, which was then ruled by the Empress Irene (i-re'-ne). After defeating Irene's famous general, Nicetas (ni-ce'-tas), Harun marched his army to Chrysopolis (Chrys-op'-o-lis), now Scutari (skoo'-ta-re), on the Asiatic coast, opposite Constantinople. He encamped on the heights, in full view of the Roman capital.

The Empress saw that the city would certainly by taken by the Moslems. She therefore sent ambassadors to Harun to arrange terms; but he sternly refused to agree to anything except immediate surrender.

Then one of the ambassadors said, "The Empress has heard much of your ability as a general. Though you are her enemy, she admires you as a soldier."

These flattering words were pleasing to Harun. He walked to and fro in front of his tent and then spoke again to the ambassadors.

"Tell the Empress," he said, "that I will spare Constantinople if she will pay me seventy thousand pieces of gold as a yearly tribute. If the tribute is regularly paid Constantinople shall not be harmed by any Moslem force."

The Empress had to agree to these terms. She paid the first year's tribute; and soon the great Moslem army set out on its homeward march.

When Harun was not quite twenty-one years old he became caliph.

He began his reign by appointing very able ministers, who carried on the work of the government so well that they greatly improved the condition of the people.

Harun built a palace in Bagdad, far grander and more beautiful than that of any caliph before him. Here he established his court and lived in great splendor, attended by hundreds of courtiers and slaves.

He was very anxious that his people should be treated justly by the officers of the government; and he was determined to find out whether any had reason to complain. So he sometimes disguised himself at night and went about through the streets and bazaars, listening to the talk of those whom he met and asking them questions. In this way he learned whether the people were contented and happy, or not.

In those times Bagdad in the east and the Mohammedan cities of Spain in the west were famed for their schools and learned men. Arabian teachers first introduced into Western Europe both algebra and the figures which we use in arithmetic. It is for this reason that we call these figures the "Arabic numerals."

Harun-al-Rashid gave great encouragement to learning. He was a scholar and poet himself and whenever he heard of learned men in his own kingdom, or in neighboring countries, he invited them to his court and treated them with respect.

The name of Harun, therefore, became known throughout the world. It is said that a correspondence took place between him and Charlemagne and that, as you have learned, Harun sent the great emperor a present of a clock and an elephant.

The tribute of gold that the Empress Irene agreed to pay Harun was sent regularly for many years. It was always received at Bagdad with great ceremony. The day on which it arrived was made a holiday. The Roman soldiers who came with it entered the gates in procession. Moslem troops also took part in the parade.

When the gold had been delivered at the palace, the Roman soldiers were hospitably entertained, and were escorted to the main gate of the city when they set out on their journey back to Constantinople.

2

In 802 Nicephorus (Ni-ceph'-o-rus) usurped the throne of the Eastern Empire. He sent ambassadors with a letter to Harun to tell him that the tribute would no longer be paid. The letter contained these words:

"The weak and faint-hearted Irene submitted to pay you tribute. She ought to have made you pay tribute to her. Return to me all that she paid you; else the matter must be settled by the sword."

As soon as Harun had read these words the ambassadors threw a bundle of swords at his feet. The caliph smiled, and drawing his own sword, or cimeter (sim'-e-ter), he cut the Roman swords in two with one stroke without injuring the bald, or even turning the edge of his weapon.

Then he dictated a letter to Nicephorus, in which he said:

"Harun-al-Rashid, Commander of the Faithful to Nicephorus, the Roman dog: I have read thy letter. Thou shalt not hear, thou shalt SEE my reply."

Harun was as good as his word. He started that day with a large army to punish the emperor. As soon as he reached Roman territory he ravaged the country and took possession of everything valuable that he found. He laid siege to Heraclea (Her-a-cle'-a), a city on the shores of the Black Sea, and in a week forced it to surrender. Then he sacked the place.

Nicephorus was now forced to agree to pay the tribute. Scarcely, however, had the caliph reached his palace in Bagdad when the emperor again refused to pay.

Harun, consequently, advanced into the Roman province of Phrygia, in Asia Minor, with an army of 15,000 men. Nicepherus marched against him with 125,000 men. In the battle which followed the emperor was wounded, and 40,000 of his men were killed.

After this defeat Nicephorus again promised payment of the tribute, but again failed to keep his promise.

Harun now vowed that he would kill the emperor if he should ever lay hands upon him. But as he was getting ready to march once more into the Roman provinces a revolt broke out in one of the cities of his own kingdom; and while on his way to suppress it the great caliph died of an illness which had long given him trouble.

Egbert. King from 802-837 A.D.

1

Egbert the Saxon lived at the same time as did Harun-al-Rashid and Charlemagne. He was the first king who ruled all England as one kingdom. Long before his birth the people who are known to us as Britons lived there, and they gave to the island the name Britain.

But Britain was invaded by the Romans under Julius Cæsar and his successors, and all that part of it which we now call England was added to the Empire of Rome. The Britons were driven into Wales and Cornwall, the western sections of the island.

The Romans kept possession of the island for nearly four hundred years. They did not leave it until 410, the year that Alaric sacked the city of Rome. At this time the Roman legions were withdrawn from Britain.

Some years before this the Saxons, Angles and Jutes, German tribes, had settled near the shores of the North Sea. They learned much about Britain; for trading vessels, even at that early day, crossed the Channel. Among other things, the men from the north learned that Britain was crossed with good Roman roads, and dotted with houses of brick and stone; that walled cities had taken the place of tented camps, and that the country for miles round each city was green every spring with waving wheat, or white with orchard blossoms.

After the Roman legions had left Britain, the Jutes, led, it is said, by two great captains named Hengist and Horsa, landed upon the southeastern coast and made a settlement.

Britain proved a pleasant place to live in, and soon the Angles and Saxons also left the North Sea shores and invaded the beautiful island.

The new invaders met with brave resistance. The Britons were headed by King Arthur, about whom many marvelous stories are told. His court was held at Caerleon (cär'-le-on), in North Wales, where his hundred and fifty knights banqueted at their famous "Round Table."

The British king and his knights fought with desperate heroism. But they could not drive back the Saxons and their companions and were obliged to seek refuge in the western mountainous parts of the island, just as their forefathers had done when the Romans invaded Britain. Thus nearly all England came into the possession of the three invading tribes.

Arthur and his knights were devoted Christians. For the Romans had not only made good roads and built strong walls and forts in Britain, but they had also brought the Christian religion into the island. And at about the time of the Saxon invasion St. Patrick was founding churches and monasteries in Ireland, and was baptizing whole clans of the Irish at a time. It is said that he baptized 12,000 persons with his own hand. Missionaries were sent out by the Irish Church to convert the wild Picts of Scotland and at a later day the distant barbarians of Germany and Switzerland.

The Saxons, Angles, and Jutes believed in the old Norse gods, and Tiew and Woden, Thor and Friga, or Frija, were worshiped on the soil of Britain for more than a hundred years.

The Britons tried to convert their conquerors, but the invaders did not care to be taught religion by those whom they had conquered; so the British missionaries found the work unusually hard. Aid came to them in a singular way. At some time near the year 575 A.D., the Saxons quarreled and fought with their friends, the Angles. They took some Angles prisoners and carried them to Rome to be sold in the great slave-market there. A monk named Gregory passed one day through the market and saw these captives. He asked the dealer who they were. "Angles," was the answer.

"Oh," said the monk, "they would be ANGELS instead of ANGLES if they were only Christians; for they certainly have the faces of angels."

Years after, when that monk was the Pope of Rome, he remembered this conversation and sent the monk Augustine (Au-gus'-tine) to England to teach the Christian religion to the savage but angel-faced Angles. Augustine and the British missionaries converted the Anglo-Saxons two hundred years before the German Saxons were converted.

Still, though both Angles and Saxons called themselves Christians, they were seldom at peace; and for more than two hundred years they frequently fought. Various chiefs tried to make themselves kings; and at length there came to be no less than seven small kingdoms in South Britain.

In 784 Egbert claimed to be heir of the kingdom called Wessex; but the people elected another man and Egbert had to flee for his life. He went to the court of Charlemagne, and was with the great king of the Franks in Rome on Christmas Day, 800, when the Pope placed the crown on Charles' head and proclaimed him emperor.

Soon after this a welcome message came to Egbert. The mind of the people in Wessex had changed and they had elected him king. So bidding farewell to Charlemagne, he hurried to England.

Egbert had seen how Charlemagne had compelled the different quarreling tribes of

Germany to yield allegiance to him and how after uniting his empire he had ruled it well.

Egbert did in England what Charlemagne had done in Germany. He either persuaded the various petty kingdoms of the Angles, the Saxons and the Jutes to recognize him as their ruler, or forced them to do so; and thus under him all England became one united kingdom.

But Egbert did even better than this. He did much to harmonize the different tribes by his wise conciliation. The name "England" is a memorial of this; for though Egbert himself was a Saxon, he advised that to please the Angles the country should be called Anglia (An'-gli-a), that is, Angleland or England, the land of the Angles, instead of Saxonia (Sax-on-i'-a), or Saxonland.

Rollo the Viking. Died 931 A.D.

1

For more than two hundred years during the Middle Ages the Christian countries of Europe were attacked on the southwest by the Saracens of Spain, and on the northwest by the Norsemen, or Northmen. The Northmen were so called because they came into Middle Europe from the north. Sometimes they were called Vikings (Vi'-kings), or pirates, because they were adventurous sea-robbers who plundered all countries which they could reach by sea.

Their ships were long and swift. In the center was placed a single mast, which carried one large sail. For the most part, however, the Norsemen depended on rowing, not on the wind, and sometimes there were twenty rowers in one vessel.

The Vikings were a terror to all their neighbors; but the two regions that suffered most from their attacks were the Island of Britain and that part of Charlemagne's empire in which the Franks were settled.

Nearly fifty times in two hundred years the lands of the Franks were invaded. The Vikings sailed up the large rivers into the heart of the region which we now call France and captured and pillaged cities and towns. Some years after Charlemagne's death they went as far as his capital, Aix (aks), took the place, and stabled their horses in the cathedral which the great emperor had built.

In the year 860 they discovered Iceland and made a settlement upon its shores. A few years later they sailed as far as Greenland, and there established settlements which existed for about a century.

These Vikings were the first discoverers of the continent on which we live. Ancient books found in Iceland tell the story of the discovery. It is related that a Viking ship was driven during a storm to a strange coast, which is thought to have been that part of America now known as Labrador.

When the captain of the ship returned home he told what he had seen. His tale so excited the curiosity of a young Viking prince, called Leif the Lucky, that he sailed to the newly discovered coast.

Going ashore, he found that the country abounded in wild grapes; and so he called it Vinland, or the land of Vines. Vinland is thought to have been a part of what is now the Rhode Island coast.

The Vikings were not aware that they had found a great unknown continent. No one in the more civilized parts of Europe knew anything about their discovery; and after a while the story of the Vinland voyages seems to have been forgotten, even among the Vikings themselves.

So it is not to them that we owe the discovery of America, but to Columbus; because his discovery, though nearly five hundred years later than that of the Norsemen, actually made known to all Europe, for all time, the existence of the New World.

2

The Vikings had many able chieftains. One of the most famous was Rollo the Walker, so called because he was such a giant that no horse strong enough to carry him could be found, and therefore he always had to walk. However, he did on foot what few could do on horseback.

In 885 seven hundred ships, commanded by Rollo and other Viking chiefs, left the harbors of Norway, sailed to the mouth of the Seine (San), and started up the river to capture the city of Paris.

Rollo and his men stopped on the way at Rouen (rö-on'), which also was on the Seine, but nearer its mouth. The citizens had heard of the giant, and when they saw the river covered by his fleet they were dismayed. However, the bishop of Rouen told them that Rollo could be as noble and generous as he was fierce; and he advised them to open their gates and trust to the mercy of the Viking chief. This was done, and Rollo marched into Rouen and took possession of it. The bishop had given good advice, for Rollo treated the people very kindly.

Soon after capturing Rouen he left the place, sailed up the river to Paris, and joined the other Viking chiefs. And now for six long miles the beautiful Seine was covered with Viking vessels, which carried an army of thirty thousand men.

A noted warrior named Eudes (Ude) was Count of Paris, and he had advised the Parisians to fortify the city. So not long before the arrival of Rollo and his companions, two walls with strong gates had been built round Paris.

It was no easy task for even Vikings to capture a strongly walled city. We are told that Rollo and his men built a high tower and rolled it on wheels up to the walls. At its top was a floor well manned with soldiers. But the people within the city shot hundreds of arrows at the besiegers, and threw down rocks, or poured boiling oil and pitch upon them.

The Vikings thought to starve the Parisians, and for thirteen months they encamped round the city. At length food became very scarce, and Count Eudes determined to go for help. He went out through one of the gates on a dark, stormy night, and rode post-haste to the king. He told him that something must be done to save the people of Paris.

So the king gathered an army and marched to the city. No battle was fought--the Vikings seemed to have been afraid to risk one. They gave up the siege, and Paris was relieved.

Rollo and his men went to the Duchy of Burgundy, where, as now, the finest crops were raised and the best of wines were made.

3

Perhaps after a time Rollo and his Vikings went home; but we do not know what he did for about twenty-five years. We do know that he abandoned his old home in Norway in 911. Then he and his people sailed from the icy shore of Norway and again went up the Seine in hundreds of Viking vessels.

Of course, on arriving in the land of the Franks, Rollo at once began to plunder towns and farms.

Charles, then king of the Franks, although his people called him the Simple, or Senseless, had sense enough to see that this must be stopped.

So he sent a message to Rollo and proposed that they should have a talk about peace. Rollo agreed and accordingly they met. The king and his troops stood on one side of a little river, and Rollo with his Vikings stood on the other. Messages passed between them. The king asked Rollo what he wanted.

"Let me and my people live in the land of the Franks; let us make ourselves home here, and I and my Vikings will become your vassals," answered Rollo. He asked for Rouen and the neighboring land. So the king gave him that part of Francia; and ever since it has been called Normandy, the land of the Northmen.

When it was decided that the Vikings should settle in Francia and be subjects of the Frankish king, Rollo was told that he must kiss the foot of Charles in token that he would be the king's vassal. The haughty Viking refused. "Never," said he, "will I bend my knee before any man, and no man's foot will I kiss." After some persuasion, however, he ordered one of his men to perform the act of homage for him. The king was on horseback and the Norseman, standing by the side of the horse, suddenly seized the king's foot and drew it up to his lips. This almost made the king fall from his horse, to the great amusement of the Norsemen.

Becoming a vassal to the king meant that if the king went to war Rollo would be obliged to join his army and bring a certain number of armed men--one thousand or more.

Rollo now granted parts of Normandy to his leading men on condition that they would bring soldiers to his army and fight under him. They became his vassals, as he was the king's vassal.

The lands granted to vassals in this way were called feuds, and this plan of holding lands was called the Feudal System.

It was established in every country of Europe during the Middle Ages.

The poorest people were called serfs. They were almost slaves and were never permitted to leave the estate to which they belonged. They did all the work. They worked chiefly for the landlords, but partly for themselves.

Having been a robber himself, Rollo knew what a shocking thing it was to ravage and plunder, and he determined to change his people's habits. He made strict laws and hanged robbers. His duchy thus became one of the safest parts of Europe.

The Northmen learned the language of the Franks and adopted their religion.

The story of Rollo is especially interesting to us, because Rollo was the forefather of that famous Duke of Normandy who, less than a hundred and fifty years later, conquered England and brought into that country the Norman nobles with their French language and customs.

Fig. 9 – Drake or drakkar, a viking ship

Alfred the Great. King from 871-901 A.D.

1

The Danes were neighbors of the Norwegian Vikings, and like them were fond of the sea and piracy. They plundered the English coasts for more than a century; and most of northern and eastern England became for a time a Danish country with Danish kings.

What saved the rest of the country to the Saxons was the courage of the great Saxon king, Alfred.

Alfred was the son of Ethelwulf, king of the West Saxons. He had a loving mother who brought him up with great care. Up to the age of twelve, it is said, he was not able to read well, in spite of the efforts of his mother and others to teach him.

When Alfred was a boy there were no printed books. The wonderful art of printing was not invented until about the year 1440--nearly six hundred years later than Alfred's time. Moreover, the art of making paper had not yet been invented. Consequently the few books in use in Alfred's time were written by skillful penmen, who wrote generally on leaves of parchment, which was sheepskin carefully prepared so that it might retain ink.

One day Alfred's mother showed him and his elder brothers a beautiful volume which contained a number of the best Saxon ballads. Some of the words in this book were written in brightly colored letters, and upon many of the leaves were painted pictures of gaily-dressed knights and ladies.

"Oh, what a lovely book!" exclaimed the boys.

"Yes, it is lovely," replied the mother. "I will give it to whichever of you children can read it the best in a week."

Alfred began at once to take lessons in reading, and studied hard day after day. His brothers passed their time in amusements and made fun of Alfred's efforts. They thought he could not learn to read as well as they could, no matter how hard he should try.

At the end of the week the boys read the book to their mother, one after the other. Much to the surprise of his brothers, Alfred proved to be the best reader and his mother gave him the book.

While still very young Alfred was sent by his father to Rome to be anointed by His Holiness, the Pope. It was a long and tiresome journey, made mostly on horseback.

With imposing, solemn ceremony he was anointed by the Holy Father. Afterwards he spent a year in Rome receiving religious instruction.

2

In the year 871, when Alfred was twenty-two years old, the Danes invaded various parts of England. Some great battles were fought, and Alfred's elder brother Ethelred, king of the West Saxons, was killed. Thus Alfred became king.

The Danes still continued to fight the Saxons, and defeated Alfred in a long and severe struggle. They took for themselves the northern and eastern parts of England.

Moreover, Danes from Denmark continued to cross the sea and ravage the coast of Saxon England. They kept the people in constant alarm. Alfred therefore determined to meet the pirates on their own element, the sea. So he built and equipped the first English navy, and in 875 gained the first naval victory ever won by the English.

A few years after this, however, great numbers of Danes from the northern part of England came pouring into the Saxon lands. Alfred himself was obliged to flee for his life.

For many months he wandered through forests and over hills to avoid being taken by the Danes. He sometimes made his home in caves and in the huts of shepherds and cowherds. Often he tended the cattle and sheep and was glad to get a part of the farmer's dinner in pay for his services.

Once, when very hungry, he went into the house of a cowherd and asked for something to eat. The cowherd's wife was baking cakes and she said she would give him some when they were done.

"Watch the cakes and do not let them burn, while I go across the field to look after the cows," said the woman, as she hurried away. Alfred took his seat on the chimney-corner to do as he was told. But soon his thoughts turned to his troubles and he forgot about the cakes.

When the woman came back she cried out with vexation, for the cakes were burned and spoiled. "You lazy, good-for-nothing man!" she said, "I warrant you can eat cakes fast enough; but you are too lazy to help me bake them."

With that she drove the poor hungry Alfred out of her house. In his ragged dress he certainly did not look like a king, and she had no idea that he was anything but a poor beggar.

3

Some of Alfred's friends discovered where he was hiding and joined him. In a little time a body of soldiers came to him and a strong fort was built by them. From this fort Alfred and his men went out now and then and gave battle to small parties of the Danes. Alfred was successful and his army grew larger and larger.

One day he disguised himself as a wandering minstrel and went into the camp of the Danes. He strolled here and there, playing on a harp and singing Saxon ballads. At last, Guthrum (Guth'-rum), the commander of the Danes, ordered the minstrel to be brought to his tent.

Alfred went. "Sing to me some of your charming songs," said Guthrum. "I never heard more beautiful music." So the kingly harper played and sang for the Dane, and went away with handsome presents. But better than that, he had gained information that was of the greatest value.

In a week he attacked the Danish forces and defeated them with great slaughter in a battle which lasted all day and far into the night. Guthrum was taken prisoner and brought before Alfred.

Taking his harp in his hands, Alfred played and sang one of the ballads with which he had entertained Guthrum in the camp. The Dane started in amazement and exclaimed:

"You, then, King Alfred, were the wandering minstrel?"

"Yes," replied Alfred, "I was the musician whom you received so kindly. Your life is now in my hands; but I will give you your liberty if you will become a Christian and never again make war on my people."

"King Alfred," said Guthrum, "I will become a Christian, and so will all my men if you will grant liberty to them as to me; and henceforth, we will be your friends."

Alfred then released the Danes, and they were baptized as Christians.

An old road running across England from London to Chester was then agreed upon as the boundary between the Danish and Saxon kingdoms; and the Danes settled in East Anglia, as the eastern part of England was called.

Years of peace and prosperity followed for Alfred's kingdom. During these years the king rebuilt the towns that had been destroyed by the Danes, erected new forts, and greatly strengthened his army and navy.

He also encouraged trade; and he founded a school like that established by Charlemagne. He himself translated a number of Latin books into Saxon, and probably did more for the cause of education than any other king that ever wore the English crown.

Henry the Fowler. King from 919-936 A.D.

1

About a hundred years had passed since the death of Charlemagne, and his great empire had fallen to pieces. Seven kings ruled where he had once been sole emperor.

West of the Rhine, where the Germans lived, the last descendant of Charlemagne died when he was a mere boy. The German nobles were not willing for any foreign prince to govern them, and yet they saw that they must unite to defend their country against the invasions of the barbarians called Magyars (ma-järz'). So they met and elected Conrad, duke of Franconia, to be their king.

However, although he became king in name, Conrad never had much power over his nobles. Some of them refused to recognize him as king and his reign was disturbed by quarrels and wars. He died in 919, and on his death-bed he said to his brother, "Henry, Duke of Saxony, is the ablest ruler in the empire. Elect him king, and Germany will have peace."

A few months after Conrad's death, the nobles met at Aix-la-Chapelle and elected Henry to be their king.

At this time it was the custom in Europe to hunt various birds, such as the wild duck and partridge, with falcons. The falcons were long-winged birds of prey, resembling hawks. They were trained to perch on their master's wrist and wait patiently until they were told to fly. Then they would swiftly dart at their prey and bear it to the ground. Henry was very fond of falconry and hence was known as Henry the Fowler, or Falconer.

As soon as the other dukes had elected him king a messenger was sent to Saxony to inform him of the honor done him. After a search of some days he was at last found, far up in the Hartz Mountains, hunting with his falcons. Kneeling at his feet, the messenger said:

"God save you, Henry of Saxony. I come to announce the death of King Conrad and to tell you that the nobles have elected you to succeed him as king of the Germans."

For a moment the duke was speechless with amazement. Then he exclaimed:

"Elected me king? I cannot believe it. I am a Saxon, and King Conrad was a Frank and a bitter enemy to me."

"It is true," replied the messenger. "Conrad, when dying, advised that the nobles should choose you as his successor."

Henry was silent for while and then he said, "King Conrad was a good man. I know it now; and I am sorry that I did not understand him better when he was alive. I accept the position offered to me and I pray that I may be guided by Heaven in ruling his people."

So Henry the Fowler left the chase to take up his duties as king of the Germans.

II

In proper time Henry was proclaimed king of Germany; but he was hardly seated on the throne when the country was invaded by thousands of Magyars, from the land which we now know as Hungary.

As soon as possible Henry gathered an army and marched to meet the barbarians. He came upon a small force under the command of the son of the Magyar king. The Germans easily routed the Magyars and took the king's son prisoner.

This proved to be a very fortunate thing, because it stopped the war for a long term of years. When the Magyar king learned that his son was a prisoner in the hands of King Henry he was overwhelmed with grief. He mourned for his son day and night and at last sent to the German camp a Magyar chief with a flag of truce, to bet that the prince might be given up.

"Our king says that he will give whatever you demand for the release of his son," said the chief to the German monarch.

"I will give up the prince on this condition only," was the reply, "the Magyars must leave the soil of Germany immediately and promise not to war on us for nine years. During those years I will pay to the king yearly five thousand pieces of gold."

"I accept the terms in the king's name," responded the chief. The prince was, therefore, given up and the Magyars withdrew.

During the nine years of truce King Henry paid great attention to the organization of an army. Before this the German soldiers had fought chiefly on foot, not, as the Magyars did, on horseback. For this reason they were at a great disadvantage in battle. The king now raised a strong force of horsemen and had them drilled so thoroughly that they became almost invincible. The infantry also were carefully drilled.

Besides this, Henry built a number of forts in different parts of his kingdom and had all the fortified cities made stronger.

The following year the Magyar chief appeared at the German court and demanded a tenth payment.

"Not a piece of gold will be given you," replied King Henry. "Our truce is ended."

In less than a week a vast body of Magyars entered Germany to renew the war. Henry held his army in waiting until lack of food compelled the barbarians to divide their forces into two separate bodies. One division was sent to one part of the country, the other to another part.

Henry completely routed both divisions, and the power of the Magyars in Germany was broken.

The Danes also invaded Henry's kingdom, but he defeated them and drove them back.

Henry reigned for eighteen years; and when he died all Germany was peaceful and prosperous. His son Otto succeeded him. He assumed the title of "Emperor," which Charlemagne had borne more than a hundred years before.

From that time on, for nearly one thousand years, all the German emperors claimed to be the successors of Charlemagne. They called their domain "the Holy Roman Empire," and took the title "Emperor" or "Emperor of the Romans," until the year 1806, when Francis II resigned it.

Canute the Great. King from 1014-1035

1

The Danes, you remember, had the eastern and northern parts of England in the time of Alfred. Alfred's successors drove them farther and farther north, and at length the Danish kingdom in England came to an end for a time.

But the Danes in Denmark did not forget that there had been such a kingdom and in the year 1013 Sweyn (swane), King of Denmark, invaded England and defeated the Anglo-Saxons. Ethelred, their king, fled to Normandy.

Sweyn now called himself the king of England; but in a short time he died and his son Canute succeeded to his throne. Canute was nineteen years old. He had been his father's companion during the war with the Anglo-Saxons, and thus had had a good deal of experience as a soldier.

After the death of Sweyn some of the Anglo-Saxons recalled King Ethelred and revolted against the Danes.

Canute, however, went to Denmark and there raised one of the largest armies of Danes that had ever been assembled. With this powerful force he sailed to England. When he landed Northumberland and Wessex acknowledged him as king. Shortly after this Ethelred died.

Canute now thought he would find it easy to get possession of all England. This was a mistake.

Ethelred left a son named Edmund Ironside who was a very brave soldier. He became, by his father's death, the king of Saxon England and at once raised an army to defend his kingdom. A battle was fought and Edmund was victorious. This was the first of five battles that were fought in one year. In none of them could the Danes do more than gain a slight advantage now and then.

However, the Saxons were at last defeated in a sixth battle through the act of a traitor. Edric, a Saxon noble, took his men out of the fight and his treachery so weakened the Saxon army that Edmund Ironside had to surrender to Canute.

But the young Dane had greatly admired Edmund for the way in which he had fought against heavy odds, so he now treated him most generously. Canute took certain portions of England and the remainder was given to Edmund Ironside.

Thus for a short time the Anglo-Saxon people had at once a Danish and a Saxon monarch.

2

Edmund died in 1016 and after his death Canute became sole ruler.

He ruled wisely. He determined to make his Anglo-Saxon subjects forget that he was a foreign conqueror. To show his confidence in them he sent back to Denmark the army he had brought over the sea, keeping on a part of his fleet and a small body of soldiers to act as guards at his palace.

He now depended on the support of his Anglo-Saxon subjects and he won their love.

Although a king--and it is generally believed that kings like flattery--Canute is said to have rebuked his courtiers when they flattered him. On one occasion, when they were talking about his achievements, one of them said to him:

"Most noble king, I believe you can do anything."

Canute sternly rebuked the courtier for these words and then said:

"Come with me, gentlemen."

He led them from the palace grounds to the sea-shore where the tide was rising, and had his chair placed at the edge of the water.

"You say I can do anything," he said to the courtiers. "Very well, I who am king and the lord of the ocean now command these rising waters to go back and not dare wet my feet."

But the tide was disobedient and steadily rose and rose, until the feet of the king were in the water. Turning to his courtiers, Canute said:

"Learn how feeble is the power of earthly kings. None is worthy the name of king but He whom heaven and earth and sea obey."

During Canute's reign England had peace and prosperity and the English people have ever held his memory dear.

The Cid

Late one sunny afternoon one and twenty knights were riding along the highway in the northern part of Spain. As they were passing a deep mire they heard cries for help, and turning, saw a poor leper who was sinking in the mud. One of the knights, a handsome young man, was touched by the cries. He dismounted, rescued the poor fellow, took him upon his own horse, and thus the two rode to the inn. The other knights wondered at this.

When they reached the inn where they were to stop for the night, they wondered still more, for their companion gave the leper a seat next to himself at the table. After supper the knight shared his own bed with the leper. If the knight had not done this, the leper would have been driven out of the town, with nothing to eat and no place in which to sleep. At midnight, while the young man was fast asleep, the leper breathed upon his back. This awakened the knight, who turned quickly in his bed and found that the leper was gone.

The knight called for a light and searched, but in vain. While he was wondering about what had happened, a man in shining garments appeared before him and said, "Rodrigo, art thou asleep or awake?" The knight answered, "I am awake, but who art thou that bringest such brightness?" The vision replied, "I am St. Lazarus, the leper to whom thou wast so kind. Because I have breathed upon thee thou shalt accomplish whatever thou shalt undertake in peace or in battle. All shall honor thee. Therefore, go on and evermore do good."

With that the vision vanished.

The promise of St. Lazarus was fulfilled. In time young Rodrigo became the great hero of Spain. The Spaniards called him Campeador (cam-pe-ä-dor'), or Champion. The Saracens called him "The Cid," or Lord. His real name was Rodrigo Diaz de Bivar, but he is usually spoken of as "The Cid."

The Goths, after the death of Alaric, had taken Spain away from the Romans. The Saracens, or, as they were usually called, the Moors, had crossed the sea from Africa and in turn had taken Spain from the Goths. In the time of Charles Martel the Goths had lost all Spain except the small mountain district in the northern part. In the time of the Cid the Goths, now called Spaniards, had driven the Moors down to about the middle of Spain. War went on all the time between the two races, and many men spent their lives in fighting. The Spanish part of the country then comprised the kingdoms of Castile, Leon, Aragon and others.

The Cid was a subject of Fernando of Castile. Fernando had a dispute with the king of Aragon about a city which each claimed. They agreed to decide the matter by a combat. Each was to choose a champion. The champions were to fight, and the king whose champion won was to have the city. Fernando chose the Cid, and though the other champion was called the bravest knight in Spain, the youthful warrior vanquished him.

When Alfonzo, a son of Fernando, succeeded to the throne, he became angry with the Cid without just cause and banished him from Christian Spain.

The Cid was in need of some money, so he filled two chests with sand and sent word to two wealthy money lenders that he wished to borrow six hundred Spanish marks (about $2,000 [as of 1904]), and would put into their hands his treasures of silver and gold which were packed in two chests, but the money lenders must solemnly swear not to open the chests until a full year had passed. To this they gladly agreed. They took the chests and loaned him six hundred marks.

The Cid was now ready for his journey. Three hundred of his knights went into banishment with him. They crossed the mountains and entered the land of the Moors. Soon they reached the town of Alcocer, and after a siege captured it and lived in it.

Then the Moorish king of Valencia ordered two chiefs to take three thousand horsemen, recapture the town and bring the Cid alive to him.

So the Cid and his men were shut up in Alcocer and besieged. Famine threatened them and they determined to cut their way through the army of the Moors. Suddenly and swiftly they poured from the gate of Alcocer, and a terrible battle was fought. The two Moorish chiefs were taken prisoners and thirteen hundred of their men were killed in the battle. The Cid then became a vassal of the Moorish king of Saragossa.

After a while Alfonzo recalled the Cid from banishment and gave him seven castles and the lands adjoining them. He needed the Cid's help in the greatest of all his plans against the Moors. He was determined to capture Toledo. He attacked it with a large army in which there were soldiers from many foreign lands. The Cid is said to have been the commander. After a long siege the city fell and the victorious army marched across the great bridge built by the Moors, which you would cross to-day if you went to Toledo. [NOTE FROM Brett Fishburne: This stunned me, so I researched it briefly and it turns out that the bridge was washed out completely in 1257, then rebuilt by Alfonso X. There were numerous other reconstructions done between then and 2000, the most recent of which I am aware was in the late 1970s using stone blocks found in situ.]

Valencia was one of the largest and richest cities in Moorish Spain. It was strongly fortified, but the Cid determined to attack it.

The plain about the city was irrigated by streams that came down from the neighboring hills. To prevent the Cid's army from coming near the city the Saracens flooded the plain. But the Cid camped on high ground above the plain and from that point besieged the city. Food became very scarce in Valencia. Wheat, barley and cheese were all so dear that none but the rich could buy them. People ate horses, dogs, cats and mice, until in the whole city only three horses and a mule were left alive.

Then on the fifteenth of June, 1094, the governor went to the camp of the Cid and delivered to him the keys of the city. The Cid placed his men in all the forts and took the citadel as his own dwelling. His banner floated from the towers. He called himself the Prince of Valencia.

When the king of Morocco heard of this he raised an army of fifty thousand men. They crossed from Africa to Spain and laid siege to Valencia. But the Cid with his men made a sudden sally and routed them and pursued them for miles. It is said that fifteen thousand soldiers were drowned in the river Guadalquivir (Gua-dal-qui-vir') which they tried to cross.

The Cid was now at the height of his power and lived in great magnificence. One of the first things he did was to repay the two friends who had lent him the six hundred marks. He was kind and just to the Saracens who had become his subjects. They were allowed to have their mosques and to worship God as they thought right.

In time the Cid's health began to fail. He could lead his men forth to battle no more. He sent an army against the Moors, but it was so completely routed that few of his men came back to tell the tale. It is said by a Moorish writer that "when the runaways reached him the Cid died of rage" (1099).

There is a legend that shortly before he died he saw a vision of St. Peter, who told him that he should gain a victory over the Saracens after his death.

So the Cid gave orders that his body should be embalmed. It was so well preserved that it seemed alive. It was clothed in a coat of mail, and the sword that had won so many battles was placed in the hand. Then it was mounted upon the Cid's favorite horse and fastened into the saddle, and at midnight was borne out of the gate of Valencia with a guard of a thousand knights.

All silently they marched to a spot where the Moorish king, with thirty-six chieftains, lay encamped, and at daylight the knights of the Cid made a sudden attack. The king awoke. It seemed to him that there were coming against him full seventy thousand knights, all dressed in robes as white as snow, and before them rode a knight, taller than all the rest, holding in his left hand a snow-white banner and in the other a sword which seemed of fire. So afraid were the Moorish chief and his men that they fled to the sea, and twenty thousand of them were drowned as they tried to reach their ships.

There is a Latin inscription near the tomb of the Cid which may be translated: *Brave and unconquered, famous in triumphs of war, Enclosed in this tomb lies Roderick the Great of Bivar.*

Fig. 10 – "El Cid", image from the History of the World, 1904

Edward the Confessor. King from 1042-1066

1

The Danish kings who followed Canute were not like him. They were cruel, unjust rulers and all the people of England hated them. So when in the year 1042 the last of them died, Edward, the son of the Saxon Ethelred, was elected king.

He is known in history as Edward the Confessor. He was a man of holy life and after his death was made a saint by the Church, with the title of "the Confessor." Though born in England, he passed the greater part of his life in Normandy as an exile from his native land. He was thirty-eight years old when he returned from Normandy to become king.

As he had lived so long in Normandy he always seemed more like a Norman than one of English birth. He generally spoke the French language and he chose Normans to fill many of the highest offices in his kingdom.

For the first eight years of his reign there was perfect peace in his kingdom, except in the counties of Kent and Essex, where pirates from the North Sea made occasional attacks.

These pirates were mostly Norwegians, whose leader was a barbarian named Kerdric. They would come sweeping down upon the Kentish coast in many ships, make a landing where there were no soldiers, and fall upon the towns and plunder them. Then, as swiftly and suddenly as they had come, they would sail away homeward, before they could be captured.

One day Kerdic's fleet arrived off the coast, and as no opposing force was visible, the pirates landed and started toward the nearest town to plunder it.

By a quick march a body of English soldiers reached the town before the pirates, and when the latter arrived they found a strong force drawn up to give them battle. A short struggle took place. More than half of the pirates were slain and the remainder were taken prisoners.

After the prisoners had been secured the English ships that were stationed on the coast attacked the pirate fleet and destroyed it.

2

Edward took part in the events upon which Shakespeare, five hundred years later, founded his famous tragedy of "Macbeth."

There lived in Scotland during his reign an ambitious nobleman named Macbeth, who invited Duncan, the King of Scotland, to his castle and murdered him. He tried to make it appear that the murder had been committed by Duncan's attendants and he caused the king's son and heir, Prince Malcolm, to flee from the land. He then made himself king of Scotland.

Malcolm hastened to England and appealed to King Edward for help.

When the king was told the number of soldiers Malcolm would probably need he gave orders for double that number to march into Scotland. Malcolm with this support attacked Macbeth, and after several well-fought battles drove the usurper from Scotland and took possession of the throne.

Edward did a great deal during his reign to aid the cause of Christianity. He rebuilt the ancient Westminster Abbey in London and erected churches and monasteries in different parts of England.

Edward was long supposed to have made many just laws, and years after his death the English people, when suffering from bad government, would exclaim, "Oh, for the good laws and customs of Edward the Confessor!" What he really did was to have the old laws faithfully carried out.

He died in 1066 and was buried in Westminster Abbey.

Fig. 11 – King Edward

William the Conqueror. King from 1066-1087

1

On the death of Edward the Confessor the throne of England was claimed by William, Duke of Normandy.

When Edward took refuge in Normandy after the Danes conquered England, he stayed at the palace of William. He was very kindly treated there, and William said that Edward had promised in gratitude that William should succeed him as king of England.

One day in the year 1066 when William was hunting with a party of his courtiers in the woods near Rouen, a noble came riding rapidly toward him shouting, "Your Highness, a messenger has just arrived from England, bearing the news that King Edward is dead and that Harold, the son of Earl Godwin, has been placed on the English throne."

William at once called his nobles together and said to them, "I must have your consent that I enforce my claim to England's throne by arms."

The barons gave their consent. So an army of sixty thousand men was collected and a large fleet of ships was built to carry this force across the channel.

During the months of preparation William sent an embassy to the English court to demand of Harold that he give up the throne. Harold refused.

Soon all England was startled by the news that William had landed on the English coast at the port of Hastings with a large force.

Harold immediately marched as quickly as possible from the north to the southern coast. In a week or so he arrived at a place called Senlac nine miles from Hastings, in the neighborhood of which town the Norman army was encamped. He took his position on a low range of hills and awaited the attack of William. His men were tired with their march, but he encouraged them and bade them prepare for battle.

On the morning of October 14, 1066, the two armies met. The Norman foot-soldiers opened the battle by charging on the English stockades. They ran over the plain to the low hills, singing a war-song at the top of their voices; but they could not carry the stockades although they tried again and again. They therefore attacked another part of the English forces.

William, clad in complete armor, was in the very front of the fight, urging on his troops. At one time a cry arose in his army that he was slain and a panic began. William drew off his helmet and rode along the lines, shouting, "I live! I live! Fight on! We shall conquer yet!"

The battle raged from morning till night. Harold himself fought on foot at the head of his army and behaved most valiantly. His men, tired as they were from their forced march, bravely struggled on hour after hour.

But at last William turned their lines and threw them into confusion. As the sun went down Harold was killed and his men gave up the fight.

From Hastings William marched toward London. On the way he received the surrender of some towns and burned others that would not surrender. London submitted and some of the nobles and citizens came forth and offered the English crown to the Norman duke. On the 25th of December, 1066, the "Conqueror," as he is always called, was crowned in Westminster Abbey by Archbishop Ealdred. Both English and Norman people were present. When the question was asked by the Archbishop, "Will you have William, Duke of Normandy, for your king?" all present answered, "We will."

2

At first William ruled England with moderation. The laws and customs were not changed, and in a few months after the battle of Hastings the kingdom was so peaceful that William left it in charge of his brother and went to Normandy for a visit.

While he was gone many of the English nobles rebelled against him, and on his return he made very severe laws and did some very harsh things. He laid waste an extensive territory, destroying all the houses upon it and causing thousands of persons to die from lack of food and shelter, because the people there had not sworn allegiance to him.

He made a law that all lights should be put out and fires covered with ashes at eight o'clock every evening, so that the people would have to go to bed then. A bell was rung in all cities and towns throughout England to warn the people of the hour. The bell was called the "curfew," from the French words "couvre feu," meaning "to cover fire."

To find out about the lands of England and their owners, so that everybody might be made to pay taxes, he appointed officers in all the towns to report what estates there were, who owned them, and what they were worth. The reports were copied into two volumes, called the "Domesday Book." This book showed that England at that time had a population of a little more than a million.

William made war on Scotland, and conquered it. During a war with the king of France the city of Mantes (mont) was burned by William's soldiers. As William rode over the ruins his horse stumbled and the king was thrown to the ground and injured. He was borne to Rouen, where he lay ill for six weeks. His sons and even his attendants abandoned him in his last hours. It is said that in his death struggle he fell from his bed to the floor, where his body was found by his servants.

Fig. 12 – William the Conqueror. From Makers of History, published in 1906

Peter the Hermit. About 1050-1115

1

During the Middle Ages the Christians of Europe used to go to the Holy Land for the purpose of visiting the tomb of Christ and other sacred places. Those who made such a journey were called "pilgrims."

Every year thousands of pilgrims--kings, nobles and people of humbler rank--went to the Holy Land.

While Jerusalem was in the hands of the Arabian caliphs who reigned at Bagdad, the Christian pilgrims were generally well treated. After about 1070, when the Turks took possession of the city, outrages became so frequent that it seemed as if it would not be safe for Christians to visit the Savior's tomb at all.

About the year 1095 there lived at Amiens (ä-me-an') France, a monk named Peter the Hermit.

Peter was present at a council of clergy and people held at Clermont in France when his Holiness, Pope Urban II, made a stirring speech. He begged the people to rescue the Holy Sepulchre and other sacred sites from the Mohammedans.

The council was so roused by his words that they broke forth into loud cries, "God wills it! God wills it!"

"It is, indeed, His will," said the Pope, "and let these words be your war-cry when you meet the enemy."

Peter listened with deep attention. Immediately after the council he began to preach in favor of a war against the Turks. With head and feet bare, and clothed in a long, coarse robe tied at the waist with a rope, he went through Italy from city to city, riding on a donkey. He preached in churches, on the streets--wherever he could secure an audience.

When Peter had gone over Italy he crossed the Alps and preached to the people of France, Germany, and neighboring countries. Everywhere he kindled the zeal of the people, and multitudes enlisted as champions of the cross.

Thus began the first of seven wars known as the "Crusades" or "Wars of the Cross," waged to rescue the Holy Land from the Mohammedans.

It is said that more than 100,000 men, women and children went on the first Crusade. Each wore on the right shoulder the emblem of the cross.

Peter was in command of one portion of this great multitude. His followers began their journey with shouts of joy and praise.

But they had no proper supply of provisions. So when passing through Hungary they plundered the towns and compelled the inhabitants to support them. This roused the anger of the Hungarians. They attacked the Crusaders and killed a great many of them.

After long delays about seven thousand of those who had started on the Crusade reached Constantinople. They were still enthusiastic and sounded their war-cry, "God wills it!" with as much fervor as when they first joined Peter's standard.

Leaving Constantinople, they went eastward into the land of the Turks. A powerful army led by the sultan met them. The Crusaders fought heroically all day long but at length were badly beaten. Only a few escaped and found their way back to Constantinople.

Peter the Hermit had left the Crusaders before the battle and returned to Constantinople. He afterwards joined the army of Godfrey of Bouillon.

Godfrey's army was composed of six divisions, each commanded by a soldier of high rank and distinction. It was a well organized and disciplined force and numbered about half a million men.

It started only a few weeks after the irregular multitude which followed Peter the Hermit, and was really the first Crusading army, for Peter's undisciplined throng could hardly be called an army.

After a long march Godfrey reached Antioch and laid siege to it.

It was believed that this Moslem stronghold could be taken in a short time; but the city resisted the attacks of the Christians for seven months. Then it surrendered.

And now something happened that none of the Crusaders had dreamed of. An army of two hundred thousand Persians arrived to help the Moslems. They laid siege to Antioch and shut up the Crusaders within its walls for weeks. However, after a number of engagements in which there was great loss of life, the Turks and Persians were at last driven away.

The way was now opened to Jerusalem. But out of the half million Crusaders who had marched from Europe less than fifty thousand were left. They had won their way at a fearful cost.

Still onward they pushed with brave hearts, until on a bright summer morning they caught the first glimpse of the Holy City in the distance. For two whole years they had toiled and suffered in the hope of reaching Jerusalem. Now it lay before them.

But it had yet to be taken. For more than five weeks the Crusaders carried on the siege. Finally, on the 15th of July, 1099, the Turks surrendered. The Moslem flag was hauled down and the banner of the cross floated over the Holy City.

A few days after the Christians had occupied Jerusalem Godfrey of Bouillon was chosen king of the Holy Land.

"I will accept the office," he said, "but no crown must be put on my head and I must never be called king. I cannot wear a crown of gold where Christ wore one of thorns nor will I be called king in the land where once lived the King of Kings."

Peter the Hermit is said to have preached an eloquent sermon on the Mount of Olives. He did not, however, remain long in Jerusalem, but after the capture of the city returned to Europe. He founded a monastery in France and within its walls passed the rest of his life.

Frederick Barbarossa. Emperor from 1152-1190

1

Frederick I was one of the most famous of German emperors. He was a tall, stalwart man of majestic appearance. He had a long red beard and so the people called him Barbarossa, or Red-Beard. He came to the throne in 1152.

At that time the province of Lombardy in northern Italy was a part of the German empire.

In 1158 Milan (mï-lan'), the chief city of Lombardy, revolted. Then over the Alps came an army of a hundred thousand German soldiers, with Frederick at their head. After a long siege the city surrendered.

But soon it revolted again. The emperor besieged it once more and once more it surrendered. Its fortifications were destroyed and many of its buildings ruined.

But even then the spirit of the Lombards was not broken. Milan and the other cities of Lombardy united in a league and defied the emperor. He called upon the German dukes to bring their men to his aid. All responded except Henry the Lion, duke of Saxony, Frederick's cousin, whom he had made duke of Bavaria also. Frederick is said to have knelt and implored Henry to do his duty, but in vain.

In his campaign against the Lombards Frederick was unsuccessful. His army was completely defeated and he was compelled to grant freedom to the cities of Lombardy. Everybody blamed Henry the Lion. The other dukes charged him with treason and he was summoned to appear before a meeting of the nobles. He failed to come and the nobles thereupon declared him guilty and took from him everything that he had, except the lands he had inherited from his father.

Frederick now devoted himself to making Germany a united nation. Two of his nobles had been quarreling for a long time and as a punishment for their conduct each was condemned, with ten of his counts and barons, to carry dogs on his shoulders from one country to another.

Frederick finally succeeded in keeping the nobles in the different provinces of Germany at peace with one another, and persuaded them to work together for the good of the whole empire. He had no more trouble with them and for many years his reign was peaceful and prosperous.

2

After the Christians had held Jerusalem for eighty-eight years, it was recaptured by the

Moslems under the lead of the famous Saladin (Sal'-a-din), in the year 1187. There was much excitement in Christendom, and the Pope proclaimed another Crusade.

Frederick immediately raised an army of Crusaders in the German Empire and with one hundred and fifty thousand men started for Palestine.

He marched into Asia Minor, attacked the Moslem forces, and defeated them in two great battles.

But before the brave old warrior reached the Holy Land his career was suddenly brought to an end. One day his army was crossing a small bridge over a river in Asia Minor. At a moment when the bridge was crowded with troops Frederick rode up rapidly.

He was impatient to join his son, who was leading the advance guard; and when he found that he could not cross immediately by the bridge, he plunged into the river to swim his horse across. Both horse and rider were swept away by the current. Barbarossa's heavy armor made him helpless and he was drowned. His body was recovered and buried at Antioch.

Barbarossa was so much loved by his people that it was said, "Germany and Frederick Barbarossa are one in the hearts of the Germans." His death caused the greatest grief among the German Crusaders. They had now little heart to fight the infidels and most of them at once returned to Germany.

In the Empire the dead hero was long mourned and for many years the peasants believed that Frederick was not really dead, but was asleep in a cave in the mountains of Germany, with his gallant knights around him. He was supposed to be sitting in his chair of state, with the crown upon his head, his eyes half-closed in slumber, his beard as white as snow and so long that it reached the ground.

"When the ravens cease to fly round the mountain," said the legend, "Barbarossa shall awake and restore Germany to its ancient greatness."

Fig. 13 – F. Barbarrosa, in a miniature from a manuscript written in 1188, Vatican Library

Henry the Second 1154-1189 and His Sons 1189-1216

1

In 1154, while Barbarossa was reigning in Germany, Henry II, one of England's greatest monarchs, came to the throne.

Henry was the son of Geoffrey Plantagenet (Plan-tag'-e-net), Count of Anjou in France, and Matilda, daughter of King Henry I and granddaughter of William the Conqueror. Count Geoffrey used to wear in his hat a sprig of the broom plant, which is called in Latin "planta genista." From this he adopted the name Plantagenet, and the kings who descended from him and ruled England for more than three hundred years are called the Plantagenets.

Henry II inherited a vast domain in France and managing this in addition England kept him very busy. One who knew him well said, "He never sits down; he is on his feet from morning till night."

His chief assistant in the management of public affairs was Thomas Becket, whom he made chancellor of the kingdom. Becket was fond of pomp and luxury, and lived in a more magnificent manner than even the king himself.

The clergy had at this time become almost independent of the king. To bring them under his authority Henry made Becket Archbishop of Canterbury, thus putting him at the head of the Church in England. The king expected that Becket would carry out all his wishes.

Becket, however, refused to do that which the king most desired and a quarrel arose between them. At last, to escape the king's anger, Becket fled to France and remained there for six years.

At the end of this time Henry invited him to come back to England. Not long after, however, the old quarrel began again. One day while Henry was sojourning in France, he cried out in a moment of passion, while surrounded by a group of knights, "Is there no one who will rid me of this turbulent priest?"

Four knights who heard him understood from this angry speech that he desired the death of Becket, and they went to England to murder the Archbishop. When they met Becket they first demanded that he should do as the king wished, but he firmly refused. At dusk that same day they entered Canterbury Cathedral, again seeking for him. "Where is the traitor, Thomas Becket?" one of them cried.

Becket boldly answered, "Here am I--no traitor, but a priest of god."

As he finished speaking the knights rushed upon him and killed him.

The people of England were horrified by this brutal murder. Becket was called a martyr and his tomb became a place of pious pilgrimage. The Pope canonized him and for years he was the most venerated of English saints.

King Henry was in Normandy when the murder occurred. He declared that he had had nothing whatever to do with it and he punished the murderers.

But from this time Henry had many troubles. His own sons rebelled against him, his barons were unfriendly, and conspiracies were formed. Henry thought that God was punishing him for the murder of Becket and so determined to do penance at the tomb of the saint.

For some distance before he reached Canterbury Cathedral where Becket was buried he walked over the road with bare head and feet. After his arrival he fasted and prayed a day and a night. The next day he put scourges into the hands of the cathedral monks and said, "Scourge me as I kneel at the tomb of the saint." The monks did as he bade them and he patiently bore the pain.

Henry finally triumphed over his enemies and had some years of peace, which he devoted to the good of England.

In the last year of his life, however, he had trouble again. The king of France and Henry's son Richard took up arms against him. Henry was defeated and was forced to grant what they wished. When he saw a list of the barons who had joined the French king he found among them the name of his favorite son John, and his heart was broken. He died a few days later.

2

Henry's eldest surviving son, Richard, was crowned at Westminster Abbey in 1190. He took the title of Richard I but is better known as "Cœur de Lion" ("the lion-hearted"), a name which was given him on account of his bravery. He had wonderful strength and his brave deeds were talked about all over the land.

With such a man for their king, the English people became devoted to chivalry, and on every field of battle brave men vied with another in brave deeds. Knighthood was often the reward of valor. Then, as now, knighthood was usually conferred upon a man by his king or queen. A part of the ceremony consisted in the sovereign's touching the kneeling subject's soldier with the flat of a sword and saying, "Arise, Sir Knight." This was called "the accolade."

Richard did not stay long in England after his coronation. In 1191 he went with Philip of

France on a Crusade.

The French and English Crusaders together numbered more than one hundred thousand men. They sailed to the Holy Land and joined an army of Christian soldiers encamped before the city of Acre. The besiegers had despaired of taking the city but when reinforced they gained fresh courage.

Cœur de Lion now performed deeds of valor which gave him fame throughout Europe. He was the terror of the Saracens. In every attack on Acre he led the Christians and when the city was captured he planted his banner in triumph on its walls.

So great was the terror inspired everywhere in the Holy Land by the name of Richard that Moslem mothers are said to have made their children quiet by threatening to send for the English king.

Every night when the Crusaders encamped, the heralds blew their trumpets, and cried three times, "Save the Holy Sepulchre!" And the Crusaders knelt and said, "Amen!"

The great leader of the Saracens was Saladin. He was a model of heroism and the two leaders, one the champion of the Christians and the other the champion of the Mohammedans, vied with each other in knightly deeds.

Just before one battle Richard rode down the Saracen line and boldly called for any one to step forth and fight him alone. No one responded to the challenge, for the most valiant of the Saracens did not dare to meet the lion-hearted king.

After the capture of Acre Richard took Ascalon (As'-ca-lon). Then he made a truce with Saladin, by which the Christians acquired the right for three years to visit the Holy City without paying for the privilege.

3

Richard now set out on his voyage home. He was wrecked, however, on the Adriatic Sea near Trieste. To get to England he was obliged to go through the lands of Leopold, duke of Austria, one of his bitterest enemies. So he disguised himself as a poor pilgrim returning from the Holy Land.

But he was recognized by a costly ring that he wore and was taken prisoner at Vienna by Duke Leopold. His people in England anxiously awaited his return, and when after a long time he did not appear they were sadly distressed. There is a legend that a faithful squire named Blondel went in search of him, as a wandering minstrel traveled for months over central Europe, vainly seeking for news of his master.

At last one day, while singing one of Richard's favorite songs near the walls of the castle where the king was confined, he heard the song repeated from a window. He recognized the voice of Richard. From the window Richard told him to let the English people and the people of Europe know where he was confined, and the minstrel immediately went upon his mission.

Soon Europe was astounded to learn that brave Richard of England, the great champion of Christendom, was imprisoned. The story of Blondel is probably not true, but what is true is that England offered to ransom Richard; that the Pope interceded for him; and that finally it was agreed that he should be given up on the payment of a very large sum of money. The English people quickly paid the ransom and Richard was freed.

The king of France had little love for Richard, and Richard's own brother John had less. Both were sorry that Cœur de Lion was at liberty.

John had taken charge of the kingdom during his brother's absence, and hoped that Richard might pass the rest of his days in the prison castle of Leopold.

As soon as Richard was released, the French king sent word to John, "The devil is loose again." And a very disappointed man was John when all England rang with rejoicing at Richard's return.

Upon the death of Richard, in 1199, Arthur, the son of his elder brother Geoffrey, was the rightful heir to the throne. John, however, seized the throne himself and cast Arthur into prison. There is a legend that he ordered Arthur's eyes to be put out with red hot irons. The jailor, however, was touched by the boy's prayer for mercy and spared him. But Arthur was not to escape his uncle long. It is said that one night the king took him out upon the Seine in a little boat, murdered him and cast his body into the river.

Besides being a king of England, John was duke of Normandy, and Philip, king of France, now summoned him to France to answer for the crime of murdering Arthur. John would not answer the summons and this gave the king of France an excuse for taking possession of Normandy. He did so, and thus this great province was lost forever to England. Nothing in France was left to John except Aquitaine (A-qui-taine'), which had come to him through his mother.

John's government was unjust and tyrannical, and the bishops and barons determined to preserve their rights and the rights of the people. They met on a plain called Runnymeade, and there forced John to sign the famous "Magna Carta" ("Great Charter").

Magna Carta is the most valuable charter ever granted by any sovereign to his people. In it King John names all the rights which belong to the citizens under a just government, and he promises that no one of these rights shall ever be taken away from any subjects of the English king. For violating this promise one English king lost his life and another lost the American colonies.

Magna Carta was signed in 1215. A year after he signed it the king died. His son, Henry III, succeeded him.

Fig. 14 – Henry II of England

Louis the Ninth. King from 1226-1270

1

After the time of Barbarossa and Richard Cœur de Lion lived another great Crusading king. This was a grandson of Philip II, named Louis IX, who became sovereign of France in 1226. He was then only eleven years old, so for some years his mother ruled the kingdom.

A few years after he had begun to reign Louis decided to make his brother Alphonse the governor of a certain part of France. The nobles of the region refused to have Alphonse as governor and invited Henry III of England to help them in a revolt.

Henry crossed to France with an army to support the rebellious nobles. He was duke of Aquitaine and Gascony; so that although he was the king in England he had to do homage to the king of France for his possessions in that country, and fight for him if called upon to do so.

Louis gathered an army and hastened to meet the English troops. He drove Henry from place to place, until at last he forced him to make terms of peace. The rebellious nobles who had invited the English king to France soon after swore allegiance to Louis and afterwards he had little trouble in his kingdom.

Once Louis was dangerously ill and his life was despaired of. Finally he was believed to be dying and his wife and chief officials gathered round his bed to await the end. Suddenly he roused himself and said in a feeble voice, "The cross! The cross!"

They laid the cross upon his heart and he clasped it fervently. For a while he slumbered. When he awoke he appeared much better. In a day or two he was entirely well. He then made a solemn vow that in thankfulness for his restoration he would go on a Crusade to the Holy Land.

Louis lived at a time when everybody was full of the Crusading spirit. A few years before he was born even the children in France and Germany started out upon a Crusade of their own. It is called in history the "Children's Crusade." Several thousand left their homes and marched toward the Mediterranean. They thought that God would open a pathway to the Holy Land for them through its waters. A number of them died of cold and hunger when trying to cross the Alps. Some reached Rome, and when the Pope saw them he told them to return home and not think of going on a Crusade until they were grown up.

It is easy to understand how in such an age people flocked to Louis' banner when he asked for volunteers to go with him on another Crusade.

In a few months forty thousand Crusaders assembled at a French port on the Mediterranean Sea. On a bright day in August, 1248, they went on board the fleet which was ready to sail. The king called to the Crusaders, "Sing in the name of God. Shout forth his praises as we sail away." Then quickly, on ship after ship, shouts of praise burst from the lips of thousands and amid the grand chorus the fleet began its voyage.

The Crusaders went to Damietta (Dam-i-et'-ta), in Egypt. Louis was so eager to land that he jumped into water up to his waist and waded ashore. He captured the city without striking a blow.

He had resolved to make war on the Moslems in Egypt rather than in the Holy Land, so when he left Damietta he marched southward.

He supposed there would be no strong force to stop his progress. However, he was mistaken, for he had not marched forty miles toward Cairo when he was attacked by a Moslem army led by the sultan of Egypt.

A great battle was fought. The Crusaders were commanded by King Louis and throughout the battle showed the utmost bravery, but they were outnumbered. Thousands were slain and the survivors retreated toward Damietta.

The Moslems pursued them and the Crusaders were obliged to surrender. Out of the forty thousand men who had left France only about six thousand now remained. Many had died of disease as well as in battle.

King Louis was among the prisoners, and the sultan of Egypt agreed to release him only upon the payment of a large ransom.

When the ransom had been paid a truce was made for ten years between Louis and the sultan, and the good king left Egypt. He then went to the Holy Land, and for four years worked to deliver Crusaders who were in Moslem prisons.

2

During the time that Louis was in the Holy Land his mother ruled France as regent. When she died he returned immediately to his kingdom and devoted himself to governing it.

In 1252 he took part in the founding of the Sorbonne, the most famous theological college of Europe from the days of St. Louis down to the time of the French Revolution.

He ruled his people so wisely and justly that it is hard to find any better king or even one equally as good in the whole line of French kings. He never wronged any man himself, or knowingly allowed any man to be wronged by others.

Near his palace there was a grand oak with wide-spreading branches, under which he used to sit on pleasant days in summer. There he received all persons who had complaints to make, rich and poor alike. Every one who came was allowed to tell his story without hindrance.

For hours Louis would listen patiently to all the tales of wrong-doing, of hardships and misery that were told him, and he would do what he could to right the wrongs of those who suffered.

When news came of some more dreadful persecutions of Christians by the Moslems in Palestine, Louis again raised an army of Crusaders and started with them for Tunis, although he was sick and feeble--so sick, indeed, that he had to be carried on a litter. Upon his arrival at Tunis he was attacked by fever and died in a few days.

He is better known to the world as Saint Louis than as Louis IX, because some years after his death Pope Boniface VIII canonized him on account of his pious life and his efforts to rescue the Holy Land from the Turks.

Robert Bruce. King from 1306-1329

The most famous king that Scotland ever had was Robert Bruce. He lived in the days when Edward I, Edward II, and Edward III were kings of England.

During the reign of Edward I the king of Scotland died and thirteen men claimed the throne. Instead of fighting to decide which of them should be king they asked Edward to settle the question. When he met the Scottish nobles and the rivals, each of whom thought that next day he would be wearing the crown, Edward told them that he would himself be their king. Just then an English army marched up. What could the nobles do but kneel at the feet of Edward and promise to be his vassals? This they did; and so Scotland became a part of Edward's kingdom and Baliol (Ba'-li-ol), one of the rivals who claimed the Scottish throne, was made the vassal king.

Some time after this Edward ordered Baliol to raise an army and help him fight the French. Baliol refused to do this, so Edward marched with an army into Scotland and took him prisoner. He was determined that the Scotch should have no more kings of their own. So he carried away the sacred stone of Scone (scoon), on which all kings of Scotland had to sit when they were crowned, and put it in Westminster Abbey in London, and there it is to this day. [NOTE FROM Brett Fishburne: As of 1994, the stone is in Edinburgh Castle.] It is underneath the chair on which the sovereigns of England always sit when the crown of England, Scotland, and Ireland is placed upon their heads. It is said to have been the very stone that Jacob used for a pillow on the night that he saw, in his dream, angels ascending and descending on the ladder that reached from earth to heaven.

Edward now supposed, as he had this sacred stone and had put King Baliol in prison, that Scotland was conquered.

But the men whom he appointed to govern the Scotch ruled unwisely and nearly all the people were discontented. Suddenly an army of Scots was raised. It was led by Sir William Wallace, a knight who was almost a giant in size. Wallace's men drove the English out of the country and Wallace was made the "Guardian of the Realm."

Edward then led a great army against him. The Scottish soldiers were nearly all on foot. Wallace arranged them in hollow squares--spearmen on the outside, bowmen within. The English horsemen dashed vainly against the walls of spear-points. But King Edward now brought his archers to the front. Thousands of arrows flew from their bows and thousands of Wallace's men fell dead. The spears were broken and the Scotch were defeated. Wallace barely escaped with his life. He was afterwards betrayed to Edward, who cruelly put him to death.

2

But the Scotch had learned what they could do and they still went on fighting for freedom, under two leaders named Robert Bruce and John Comyn. Edward marched against them with another large army. He won a great victory, and the nobles once more swore to obey him.

But in spite of this oath, Bruce meant to free Scotland if he could, and win the crown. He was privately crowned king of Scotland in the Abbey of Scone in 1306.

He said to his wife, "Henceforth you are the queen and I am the king of our country."

"I fear," said his wife, "that we are only playing at being king and queen, like children in their games."

"Nay, I shall be king in earnest," said Bruce.

The news that Bruce had been crowned roused all Scotland and the people took up arms to fight under him against the English. But again King Edward defeated the Scotch and Bruce himself fled to the Grampian Hills.

For two months he was closely pursued by the English who used bloodhounds to track him. He and his followers had many narrow escapes. Once he had to scramble barefoot up some steep rocks, and another time all the party would have been captured had not Bruce awakened just in time to hear the approach of the enemy. He and his men lived by hunting and fishing.

However, many brave patriots joined them, until after a while Bruce had a small army. Five times he attacked the English, and five times he was beaten. After his last defeat he fled from Scotland and took refuge in a wretched hut on an island off the north coast of Ireland. Here he stayed all alone during one winter.

3

It is said that one day, while he was very down-hearted, he saw a spider trying to spin a web between two beams of his hut. The little creature tried to throw a thread from one beam to another, but failed. Not discouraged, it tried four times more without success.

"Five times has the spider failed," said Bruce. "That is just the number of times the English have defeated me. If the spider has courage to try again, I also will try to free Scotland!"

He watched the spider. It rested for a while as if to gain strength, and then threw its slender thread toward the beam. This time it succeeded.

"I thank God!" exclaimed Bruce. "The spider has taught me a lesson. No more will I be discouraged."

About this time Edward I died and his son, Edward II, succeeded to the throne of England. For about two years the new king paid little attention to Scotland.

Meantime Bruce captured nearly all the Scotch castles that were held by the English, and the nobles and chiefs throughout the country acknowledged him as their king.

At last Edward II marched into Scotland at the head of a hundred thousand men. Bruce met him at Bannockburn on June 24, 1314, with thirty thousand soldiers.

Before the battle began Bruce rode along the front of his army to encourage his men. Suddenly an English knight, Henry de Bohun, galloped across the field and tried to strike him down with a spear. Bruce saw his danger in time and with a quick stroke of his battle-axe cleft the knight's skull.

The Scotch army shouted again and again at this feat of their commander, and they went into the battle feeling sure that the victory would be theirs. They rushed upon the English with fury and although outnumbered three to one, completely defeated them. Thousands of the English were slain and a great number captured.

In spite of this terrible blow Edward never gave up his claim to the Scottish crown. But his son Edward III, in 1328, recognized Scotland's independence and acknowledged Bruce as her king.

Marco Polo. Lived from 1254-1324

1

Some years before St. Louis led his last Crusade there was born in Venice a boy named Marco Polo. His father was a wealthy merchant who often went on trading journeys to distant lands.

In 1271, when Marco was seventeen years old, he accompanied his father and uncle on a journey through the Holy Land, Persia and Tartary, and at length to the Empire of China--then called Cathay (Ca-thay'). It took the travelers three years to reach Cathay.

The emperor of Cathay was a monarch named Kublai Khan (koo' bli-kän'), who lived in Peking.

Marco's father and uncle had been in Cathay once before and had entertained Kublai Khan by telling him about the manners and customs of Europe.

So when the two Venetian merchants again appeared in Peking, Kublai Khan was glad to see them. He was also greatly pleased with the young Marco, whom he invited to the palace.

Important positions at the Chinese court were given to Marco's father and uncle, and so they and Marco lived in the country for some years. Marco studied the Chinese language, and it was not very long before he could speak it.

When he was about twenty-one Kublai Khan sent him on very important business to a distant part of China. He did the work well and from that time was often employed as an envoy of the Chinese monarch. His travels were sometimes in lands never before visited by Europeans and he had many strange adventures among the almost unknown tribes of Asia. Step by step he was promoted. For several years he was governor of a great Chinese city.

Finally he and his father and uncle desired to return to Venice. They had all served Kublai Khan faithfully and he had appreciated it and given them rich rewards; but he did not wish to let them go.

While the matter was being talked over an embassy arrived in Peking from the king of Persia. This monarch desired to marry the daughter of Kublai Khan, the Princess Cocachin, and he had sent to ask her father for her hand. Consent was given, and Kublai Khan fitted out a fleet of fourteen ships to carry the wedding party to Persia.

The Princess Cocachin was a great friend of Marco Polo, and urged her father to allow him to go with the party. Finally Kublai Khan gave his consent. Marco's father and uncle were also allowed to go, and the three Venetians left China.

The fleet with the wedding party on board sailed southward on the China Sea. It was a long and perilous voyage. Stops were made at Borneo, Sumatra, Ceylon and other places, until the ships entered the Persian Gulf and the princess was safely landed. After they reached the capital of Persia the party, including the three Venetians, was entertained by the Persians for weeks in a magnificent manner and costly presents were given to all.

At last the Venetians left their friends, went to the Black Sea and took ship for Venice.

They had been away so long and were so much changed in appearance that none of their relations and old friends knew them when they arrived in Venice. As they were dressed in Tatar costume and sometimes spoke the Chinese language to one another, they found it hard to convince people that they were members of the Polo family.

At length, on order to show that they were the men that they declared themselves to be, they gave a dinner to all their relations and old friends. When the guests arrived they were greeted by the travelers, arrayed in gorgeous Chinese robes of crimson satin. After the first course they appeared in crimson damask; after the second, they changed their costumes to crimson velvet; while at the end of the dinner they appeared in the usual garb of wealthy Venetians.

"Now, my friends," said Marco, "I will show you something that will please you." He then brought into the room the rough Tatar coats which he and his father and uncle had worn when they reached Venice. Cutting open the seams, he took from inside the lining packets filled with rubies, emeralds and diamonds. It was the finest collection of jewels ever seen in Venice.

The guests were now persuaded that their hosts were indeed what they claimed to be.

2

Eight hundred years before Marco Polo's birth, some of the people of North Italy had fled before the Attila to the muddy islands of the Adriatic and founded Venice upon them. Since then the little settlement had become the most wealthy and powerful city of Europe. Venice was the queen of the Adriatic and her merchants were princes. They had vessels to bring the costly wares of the East to their wharves; they had warships to protect their rich cargoes from the pirates of the Mediterranean; they carried on wars. At the time when Marco Polo returned from Cathay they were at war with Genoa (Gen'-o-a).

The two cities were fighting for the trade of the world. In a great naval battle the Venetians were completely defeated. Marco Polo was in the battle and with many of his countrymen was captured by the enemy. For a year he was confined in a Genoese prison.

One of his fellow-prisoners was a skillful penman and Marco dictated to him an account of his experiences in China, Japan, and other Eastern countries. This account was carefully written out. Copies of the manuscript exist to this day. One of these is in a library in Paris. It was carried into France in the year 1307. Another copy is preserved in the city of Berne. It is said that the book was translated into many languages, so that people in all parts of Europe learned about Marco's adventures. About a hundred and seventy-five years after the book was written, the famous Genoese, Christopher Columbus, planned his voyage across the Atlantic. It is believed that he had read Marco's description of Java, Sumatra and other East India Islands, which he thought he had reached when he discovered Haiti (Hai'-ti) and Cuba. So Marco Polo may have suggested to Columbus the voyage which led to the discovery of America.

Fig. 15 – Marco Polo

Edward the Black Prince. Lived from 1330-1376

1

One of the most famous warriors of the Middle Ages was Edward the Black Prince. He was so called because he wore black armor in battle.

The Black Prince was the son of Edward III who reigned over England from 1327 to 1377. He won his fame as a soldier in the wars which his father carried on against France.

You remember that the early kings of England, from the time of William the Conqueror, had possessions in France. Henry II, William's grandson, was the duke of Normandy and lord of Brittany and other provinces, and when he married Eleanor of Aquitaine she brought him that province also.

Henry's son John lost all the French possessions of the English crown except a part of Aquitaine, and Edward III inherited this. So when Philip of Valois (val-wah') became king of France, about a year after Edward had become king of England, Edward had to do homage to Philip.

To be king of England and yet to do homage to the king of France--to bend the knee before Philip and kiss his foot--was something Edward did not like. He thought it was quite beneath his dignity, as his ancestor Rollo had thought when told that he must kiss the foot of King Charles.

So Edward tried to persuade the nobles of France that he himself ought by right to be the king of France instead of being only a vassal. Philip of Valois was only a cousin of the late French King Charles IV. Edward was the son of his sister. But there was a curious old law in France, called the Salic Law, which forbade that daughters should inherit lands. This law barred the claim of Edward, because his claim came through his mother. Still he determined to win the French throne by force of arms.

A chance came to quarrel with Philip. Another of Philip's vassals rebelled against him, and Edward helped the rebel. He hoped by doing so to weaken Philip and more easily overpower him.

Philip at once declared that Edward's possessions in France were forfeited.

Then Edward raised an army of thirty thousand men, and with it invaded France.

The Black Prince was now only about sixteen years of age, but he had already shown himself brave in battle, and his father put him in command of one of the divisions of the army.

Thousands of French troops led by King Philip were hurried from Paris to meet the advance of the English; and on the 26th of August, 1346, the two armies fought a hard battle at the village of Crécy.

During the battle the division of the English army commanded by the Black Prince had to bear the attack of the whole French force. The prince fought so bravely and managed his men so well that King Edward, who was overlooking the field of battle from a windmill on the top of a hill, sent him words of praise for his gallant work.

Again and again the prince's men drove back the French in splendid style. But at last they seemed about to give way before a very fierce charge, and the earl of Warwick hastened to Edward to advise him to send the prince aid.

"Is my son dead or unhorsed or so wounded that he cannot help himself?" asked the king.

"No, Sire," was the reply; "but he is hard pressed."

"Return to your post, and come not to me again for aid so long as my son lives," said the king. "Let the boy prove himself a true knight and win his spurs."

The earl went to the prince and told him what his father had said. "I will prove myself a true knight," exclaimed the prince. "My father is right. I need no aid. My men will hold their post as long as they have strength to stand."

Then he rode where the battle was still furiously raging, and encouraged his men. The king of France led his force a number of times against the prince's line, but could not break it and was at last compelled to retire.

The battle now went steadily against the French, although they far outnumbered the English. Finally, forty thousand of Philip's soldiers lay dead upon the field and nearly all the remainder of his army was captured. Philip gave up the struggle and fled. Among those who fought on the side of the French at Crécy was the blind king of Bohemia, who always wore three white feathers in his helmet. When the battle was at its height the blind king had his followers lead him into the thick of the fight, and he dealt heavy blows upon his unseen foes until he fell mortally wounded. The three white feathers were taken from his helmet by the Black Prince, who ever after wore them himself.

As soon as he could King Edward rode over the field to meet his son. "Prince," he said, as he greeted him, "you are the conqueror of the French." Turning to the soldiers, who had gathered around him, the king shouted, "Cheer, cheer for the Black Prince! Cheer for the hero of Crécy!"

What cheering then rose on the battle-field! The air rang with the name of the Black Prince.

Soon after the battle of Crécy King Edward laid siege to Calais; but the city resisted his attack for twelve months. During the siege the Black Prince aided his father greatly.

After the capture of Calais, it was agreed to stop fighting for seven years, and Edward's army embarked for England.

2

In 1355 Edward again declared war against the French. The Black Prince invaded France with an army of sixty thousand men. He captured rich towns and gathered a great deal of booty. While he was preparing to move on Paris, the king of France raised a great army and marched against him.

The Black Prince had lost so many men by sickness that he had only about ten thousand when he reached the city of Poitiers. Suddenly, near the city, he was met by the French force of about fifty-five thousand, splendidly armed and commanded by the king himself.

"God help us!" exclaimed the prince, when he looked at the long lines of the French as they marched on a plain before him.

Early on the morning of September 14, 1356, the battle began. The English were few in number, but they were determined to contest every inch of the ground and not surrender while a hundred of them remained to fight. For hours they withstood the onset of the French. At last a body of English horsemen charged furiously on one part of the French line, while the Black Prince attacked another part.

This sudden movement caused confusion among the French. Many of them fled from the field. When the Black Prince saw this he shouted to his men, "Advance, English banners, in the name of God and St. George!" His army rushed forward and the French were defeated. Thousands of prisoners were taken, including the king of France and many of his nobles.

The king was sent to England, where he was treated with the greatest kindness. When, some time afterwards there was a splendid procession in London to celebrate the victory of Poitiers, he was allowed to ride in the procession on a beautiful white horse, while the Black Prince rode on a pony at his side.

The Black Prince died in 1376. He was sincerely mourned by the English people. They felt that they had lost a prince who would have made a great and good king.

William Tell and Arnold von Winkelried

1

Far up among the Alps, in the very heart of Switzerland, are three districts, or cantons, as they are called, which are known as the Forest Cantons and are famous in the world's history. About two thousand years ago the Romans found in these cantons a hardy race of mountaineers, who, although poor, were free and proud of their independence. They became the friends and allies of Rome, and the cantons were a part of the Roman Empire for many years, but the people always had the right to elect their own officers and to govern themselves.

When Goths and the Vandals and the Huns from beyond the Rhine and the Danube overran the Roman Empire, these three cantons were not disturbed. The land was too poor and rocky to attract men who were fighting for possession of the rich plains and valleys of Europe, and so it happened that for century after century, the mountaineers of these cantons lived on in their old, simple way, undisturbed by the rest of the world.

In a canton in the valley of the Rhine lived the Hapsburg family, whose leaders in time grew to be very rich and powerful. They became dukes of Austria and some of them were elected emperors. One of the Hapsburgs, Albert I, claimed that the land of the Forest Cantons belonged to him. He sent a governor and a band of soldiers to those cantons and made the people submit to his authority.

In one of the Forest Cantons lived a famous mountaineer named William Tell. He was tall and strong. In all Switzerland no man had a foot so sure as his on the mountains or a hand so skilled in the use of a bow. He was determined to resist the Austrians.

Secret meetings of the mountaineers were held and all took a solemn oath to stand by each other and fight for their freedom; but they had no arms and were simple shepherds who had never been trained as soldiers. The first thing to be done was to get arms without attracting the attention of the Austrians. It took nearly a year to secure spears, swords, and battle-axes and distribute them among the mountains. Finally this was done, and everything was ready. All were waiting for a signal to rise.

The story tells us that just at this time Gessler, the Austrian governor, who was a cruel tyrant, hung a cap on a high pole in the market-place in the village of Altorf, and forced everyone who passed to bow before it. Tell accompanied by his little son, happened to pass through the marketplace. He refused to bow before the cap and was arrested. Gessler offered to release him if he would shoot an apple from the head of his son. The governor hated Tell and made this offer hoping that the mountaineer's hand would tremble and that he would kill his own son. It is said that Tell shot the apple from his son's head but that Gessler still refused to release him. That night as Tell was being carried across the lake to prison a storm came up. In the midst of the storm he sprang from the boat to an over-hanging rock and made his escape. It is said that he killed the tyrant. Some people do not believe this story, but the Swiss do, and if you go to Lake Lucerne some day they will show you the very rock upon which Tell stepped when he sprang from the boat.

That night the signal fires were lighted on every mountain and by the dawn of day the village of Altorf was filled with hardy mountaineers, armed and ready to fight for their liberty. A battle followed and the Austrians were defeated and driven from Altorf. This victory was followed by others.

A few years later, the duke himself came with a large army, determined to conquer the mountaineers. He had to march through a narrow pass, with mountains rising abruptly on either side. The Swiss were expecting him and hid along the heights above the pass, as soon as the Austrians appeared in the pass, rocks and trunks of trees were hurled down upon them. Many were killed and wounded. Their army was defeated, and the duke was forced to recognize the independence of the Forest Cantons.

This was the beginning of the Republic of Switzerland. In time five other cantons joined them in a compact for liberty.

2

About seventy years later the Austrians made another attempt to conquer the patriots. They collected a splendid army and marched into the mountains. The Swiss at once armed themselves and met the Austrians at a place called Sempach. In those times powder had not been invented, and men fought with spears, swords, and battle-axes. The Austrian soldiers stood shoulder to shoulder, each grasping a long spear whose point projected far in front of him. The Swiss were armed with short swords and spears and it was impossible for them to get to the Austrians. For a while their cause looked hopeless, but among the ranks of the Swiss was a brave man from one of the Forest Cantons. His name was Arnold von Winkelried (Win'-kel-ried). As he looked upon the bristling points of the Austrian spears, he saw that his comrades had no chance to win unless an opening could be made in that line. He determined to make such an opening even at the cost of his life. Extending his arms as far as he could, he rushed toward the Austrian line and gathered within his arms as many spears as he could grasp.

"Make way for liberty!" he cried-- Then ran, with arms extended wide, As if his dearest friend to clasp; Ten spears he swept within his grasp. "Make way for liberty!" he cried-- Their keen points met from side to side. He bowed among them like a tree, And thus made way for liberty.

Pierced through and through Winkelried fell dead, but he had made a gap in the Austrian line, and into this gap rushed the Swiss patriots. Victory was theirs and the Cantons were free.

Fig. 16 – William Tell monument, in Switerzland.

Tamerlane. Lived from 1333-1405

1

Tamerlane was the son of the chief of a Mongolian tribe in Central Asia. His real name was Timour, but as he was lamed in battle when a youth he was generally called Timour the Lame, and this name was gradually changed to Tamerlane. He was born in 1333, so that he lived in the time of the English king, Edward III, when the Black Prince was winning his victories over the French. He was a descendant of a celebrated Tatar soldier, Genghis (jen'-ghis) Khan, who conquered Persia, China, and other countries of Asia. When twenty-four years old Tamerlane became the head of his tribe, and in a few years he made himself the leader of the whole Mongolian race.

He was a tall, stern-looking man, of great strength, and, although lame in his right leg, could ride a spirited horse at full gallop and do all the work of an active soldier. He was as brave as a lion--and as cruel.

He chose the ancient city of Samarcand (Sa-mar-cand'), in Turkistan (Tur-kis-tan'), for his capital; and here he built a beautiful marble palace, where he lived in the greatest luxury.

After he had enjoyed for some time the honors which fell to him as chief ruler of the Mongolians, he began to desire further conquests. He determined to make himself master of all the countries of Central Asia.

"As there is but one God in heaven," he said, "there ought to be but one ruler on the earth."

So he gathered an immense army from all parts of his dominion, and for weeks his subjects were busy making preparations for war. At length he started for Persia in command of a splendid army. After gaining some brilliant victories he forced the Persian king to flee from his capital.

All the rich country belonging to Persia, from the Tigris to the Euphrates, submitted to the Mongolian conqueror.

Tamerlane celebrated his Persian conquest by magnificent festivities which continued for a week. Then orders were given to march into the great Tatar empire of the North. Here Tamerlane was victorious over the principal chiefs and made them his vassals. In pursuing the Tatars he entered Russia and sacked and burned some of the Russian cities. He did not, however, continue his invasion of this country, but turned in the direction of India.

At last his army stood before the city of Delhi, and after a fierce assault forced it to surrender. Other cities of India were taken and the authority of Tamerlane was established over a large extent of the country.

2

Bajazet (baj-a-zet'), sultan of Turkey, now determined to stop Tamerlane's eastward march.

News of this reached the conqueror's ears. Leaving India, he marched to meet the sultan. Bajazet was a famous warrior. He was so rapid in his movements in war that he was called "the lightning."

Tamerlane entered the sultan's dominions and devastated them. He stormed Bagdad, and after capturing the place killed thousands of the inhabitants.

At length the rivals and their armies faced each other. A great battle followed. It raged four or five hours and then the Turks were totally defeated. Bajazet was captured.

Tamerlane then ordered a great iron cage to be made and forced the sultan to enter it. The prisoner was chained to the iron bars of the cage and was thus exhibited to the Mongol soldiers, who taunted him as he was carried along the lines.

As the army marched from place to place the sultan in his cage was shown to the people. How long the fallen monarch had to bear this humiliating punishment is not known.

Tamerlane's dominions now embraced a large part of Asia. He retired to his palace at Samarcand and for several weeks indulged in festivities.

He could not, however, long be content away from the field of battle. So he made up his mind to invade the Empire of China. At the head of a great army of two hundred thousand soldiers he marched from the city of Samarcand towards China. He had gone about three hundred miles on the way when, in February, 1405, he was taken sick and died. His army was disbanded and all thought of invading China was given up.

Thus passed away one of the greatest conquerors of the Middle Ages. He was a soldier of genius but he cannot be called a truly great man. His vast empire speedily fell to pieces after his death. Since his day there has been no leader like him in that part of Asia.

Henry V. King from 1413-1422

1

Of all the kings that England ever had Henry V was perhaps the greatest favorite among the people. They liked him because he was handsome and brave and, above all, because he conquered France.

In his youth, Prince Hal, as the people called him, had a number of merry companions who sometimes got themselves into trouble by their pranks. Once one of them was arrested and brought before the chief justice of the kingdom.

Prince Hal was not pleased because sentence was given against his companion and he drew his sword, threatening the judge. Upon this the judge bravely ordered the prince to be arrested and put into prison.

Prince Hal submitted to his punishment with good grace and his father is reported to have said, "Happy is the monarch who has so just a judge, and a son so willing to obey the law."

One of Prince Hal's companions was a fat old knight named Sir John Falstaff. Once Falstaff was boasting that he and three men had beaten and almost killed two men in buckram suits who had attacked and tried to rob them. The prince led him on and gave him a chance to brag as much as he wanted to, until finally Falstaff swore that there were at least a hundred robbers and that he himself fought with fifty. Then Prince Hal told their companions that only two men had attacked Falstaff and his friends, and that he and another man who was present were those two. And he said that Falstaff, instead of fighting, had run as fast as his legs could carry him.

There was real goodness as well as merriment in Prince Hal. And so the people found; for when he became king on the death of his father he told his wild companions that the days of his wildness were over; and he advised them to lead better lives in future.

As Henry V, Prince Hal made himself famous in English history by his war with France.

Normandy, you remember, had belonged to Henry's ancestor, William the Conqueror. It had been taken from King John of England by the French king, Philip Augustus, in 1203.

Soon after his coronation Henry sent a demand to the French king that Normandy should be restored, and he made the claim which his great-grandfather, Edward III, had made that he was by right the king of France.

Of course, the king of France would not acknowledge this. Henry therefore raised an army of thirty thousand men and invaded France.

Before he began to attack the French he gave strict orders to his men that they were to harm no one who was not a soldier and to take nothing from the houses or farms of any persons who were not fighting.

Sickness broke out among Henry's troops after they landed, so that their number was reduced to about fifteen thousand. Fifty or sixty thousand Frenchmen were encamped on the field of Agincourt (äzh-an-koor') to oppose this little army.

The odds were greatly against Henry. The night before the battle one of his officers said he wished that the many thousand brave soldiers who were quietly sleeping in their beds in England were with the king.

"I would not have a single man more," said Henry. "If god give us victory, it will be plain we owe it to His grace. If not, the fewer we are the less loss for England."

The men drew courage from their king. The English archers poured arrows into the ranks of their opponents; and although the French fought bravely, they were completely routed. Eleven thousand Frenchmen fell. Among the slain were more than a hundred of the nobles of the land.

2

Agincourt was not the last of Henry's victories. He brought a second army of forty thousand men over to France. Town after town was captured, and at last Henry and his victorious troops laid siege to Rouen, which was then the largest and richest city in France.

The fortifications were so strong that Henry could not storm them, so he determined to take the place by starving the garrison. He said, "War has three handmaidens--fire, blood, and famine. I have chosen the meekest of the three."

He had trenches dug round the town and placed soldiers in them to prevent citizens from going out of the city for supplies, and to prevent the country people from taking provisions in.

A great number of the country people had left their homes when they heard that the English army was marching towards Rouen, and had taken refuge within the city walls. After the siege had gone on for six months there was so little food left in the place that the commander of the garrison ordered these poor people to go back to their homes.

Twelve thousand were put outside the gates, but Henry would not allow them to pass through his lines; so they starved to death between the walls of the French and the trenches of the English.

As winter came on the suffering of the citizens was terrible. At last they determined to set fire to the city, open their gates, and make a last desperate attack on the English.

Henry wished to preserve the city and offered such generous terms of surrender that the people accepted them. Not only Rouen but the whole of Normandy, which the French had held for two hundred years, was now forced to submit to Henry.

The war continued for about two years more, and the English gained possession of such a large part of France that at Christmas Henry entered Paris itself in triumph.

But, strange to say, the king against whom he had been fighting and over whom he was triumphing sat by his side as he rode through the streets. What did this mean? It meant that the French were so terrified by the many victories of Henry that all--king and people--were willing to give him whatever he asked. A treaty was made that as the king was feeble Henry should be regent of the kingdom and that when the king died Henry should succeed him as king of France.

In the treaty the French king also agreed to give to Henry his daughter, the Princess Katherine, in marriage. She became the mother of the English King, Henry VI.

The arrangement that an English sovereign should be king of France was never put into effect; for in less than two years after the treaty was signed the reign of the great conqueror came to an end. Henry died.

In the reign of his son all his work in gaining French territory was undone. By the time that Henry VI was twenty years old England, as you will read in the story of Joan of Arc, had nothing left of all that had been won by so many years of war except the single town of Calais.

Joan of Arc. Lived from 1412-1431

1

In the long wars between the French and English not even the Black Prince or King Henry V gained such fame as did a young French peasant girl, Joan of Arc.

She was born in the little village of Domrémy (dom-re-me'). Her father had often told her of the sad condition of France--how the country was largely in the possession of England, and how the French king did not dare to be crowned.

And so the thought came to be ever in her mind, "How I pity my country!" She brooded over the matter so much that by and by she began to have visions of angels and heard strange voices, which said to her, "Joan, you can deliver the land from the English. go to the relief of King Charles."

At last these strange visions and voices made the young girl believe that she had a mission from God, and she determined to try to save France.

When she told her father and mother of her purpose, they tried to persuade her that the visions of angels and the voices telling her of the divine mission were but dreams. "I tell thee, Joan," said her father, "it is thy fancy. Thou hadst better have a kind husband to take care of thee, and do some work to employ thy mind."

"Father, I must do what God has willed, for this is no work of my choosing," she replied. "Mother, I would far rather sit and spin by your side than take part in war. My mission is no dream. I know that I have been chosen by the Lord to fulfill His purpose and nothing can prevent me from going where He purposes to send me."

The village priest, her young companions, even the governor of the town, all tried to stop her, but it was in vain.

To the governor she said, "I must do the work my Lord has laid out for me."

Little by little people began to believe in her mission. At last all stopped trying to discourage her and some who were wealthy helped her to make the journey to the town of Chinon (she-non'), where the French king, Charles the Seventh, was living.

2

When Joan arrived at Chinon, a force of French soldiers was preparing to go to the south of France to relieve the city of Orleans which the English were besieging.

King Charles received Joan kindly and listened to what she had to say with deep attention. The girl spoke modestly, but with a calm belief that she was right.

"Gracious King," she said, "my name is Joan. God has sent me to deliver France from her enemies. You shall shortly be crowned in the cathedral of Rheims (remz). I am to lead the soldiers you are about to send for the relief of Orleans. So God has directed and under my guidance victory will be theirs."

The king and his nobles talked the matter over and finally it was decided to allow Joan to lead an army of about five thousand men against the English at Orleans.

When she left Chinon at the head of her soldiers, in April, 1429, she was in her eighteenth year. Mounted on a fine war-horse and clad in white armor from head to foot, she rode along past the cheering multitude, "seeming rather," it has been said, "of heaven than earth." In one hand she carried an ancient sword that she had found near the tomb of a saint, and in the other a white banner embroidered with lilies.

The rough soldiers who were near her left off their oaths and coarse manners, and carefully guarded her. She inspired the whole army with courage and faith as she talked about her visions.

When she arrived at the besieged city of Orleans she fearlessly rode round its walls, while the English soldiers looked on in astonishment. She was able to enter Orleans, despite the efforts of the besiegers to prevent her.

She aroused the city by her cheerful, confident words and then led her soldiers forth to give battle to the English. Their success was amazing. One after another the English forts were taken.

When only the strongest remained and Joan was leading the attacking force, she received a slight wound and was carried out of the battle to be attended by a surgeon. Her soldiers began to retreat. "Wait," she commanded, "eat and drink and rest; for as soon as I recover I will touch the walls with my banner and you shall enter the fort." In a few minutes she mounted her horse again and riding rapidly up to the fort, touched it with her banner. Her soldier almost instantly carried it. The very next day the enemy's troops were forced to withdraw from before the city and the siege was at end.

The French soldiers were jubilant at the victory and called Joan the "Maid of Orleans." By this name she is known in history. Her fame spread everywhere, and the English as well as the French thought she had more than human power.

She led the French in several other battles, and again and again her troops were victorious.

At last the English were driven far to the north of France. Then Charles, urged by Joan, went to Rheims with twelve thousand soldiers, and there, with splendid ceremonies, was crowned king. Joan holding her white banner, stood near Charles during the coronation.

When the ceremony was finished, she knelt at his feet and said, "O King, the will of God is done and my mission is over! Let me now go home to my parents."

But the king urged her to stay a while longer, as France was not entirely freed from the English. Joan consented, but she said, "I hear the heavenly voices no more and I am afraid."

However she took part in an attack upon the army of the Duke of Burgundy, but was taken prisoner by him. For a large sum of money the duke delivered her into the hands of the English, who put her in prison in Rouen. She lay in prison for a year, and finally was charged with sorcery and brought to trial. It was said that she was under the influence of the Evil One. She declared to her judges her innocence of the charge and said, "God has always been my guide in all that I have done. The devil has never had power over me."

Her trial was long and tiresome. At its close she was doomed to be burned at the stake.

So in the market-place at Rouen the English soldiers fastened her to a stake surrounded by a great pile of fagots.

A soldier put into her hands a rough cross, which he had made from a stick that he held. She thanked him and pressed it to her bosom. Then a good priest, standing near the stake, read to her the prayers for the dying, and another mounted the fagots and held towards her a crucifix, which she clasped with both hands and kissed. When the cruel flames burst out around her, the noble girl uttered the word "Jesus," and expired.

A statue of her now stands on the spot where she suffered.

Among all the men of her time none did nobler work than Joan. And hence it is that we put the story of her life among the stories of the lives of the great MEN of the Middle Ages, although she was only a simple peasant girl.

Fig. 17 – Joan of Arc, miniature painted between 1450 and 1500. Centre Historique des Archives Nationales, Paris, AE II 2490.

Gutenberg. Lived from 1400-1468

1

While Joan of Arc was busy rescuing France from the English, another wonderful worker was busy in Germany. This was John Gutenberg, who was born in Mainz.

The Germans--and most other people--think that he was the inventor of the art of printing with movable types. And so in the cities of Dresden and Mainz his countrymen have put up statues in his memory.

Gutenberg's father was a man of good family. Very likely the boy was taught to read. But the books from which he learned were not like ours; they were written by hand. A better name for them than books is "manuscripts," which means "hand-writings."

While Gutenberg was growing up a new way of making books came into use, which was a great deal better than copying by hand. It was what is called block-printing. The printer first cut a block of hard wood the size of the page that he was going to print. Then he cut out every word of the written page upon the smooth face of his block. This had to be very carefully done. When it was finished the printer had to cut away the wood from the sides of every letter. This left the letters raised, as the letters are in books now printed for the blind.

The block was now ready to be used. The letters were inked, paper was laid upon them and pressed down.

With blocks the printer could make copies of a book a great deal faster than a man could write them by hand. But the making of the blocks took a long time, and each block would print only one page.

Gutenberg enjoyed reading the manuscripts and block books that his parents and their wealthy friends had; and he often said it was a pity that only rich people could own books. Finally he determined to contrive some easy and quick way of printing.

He did a great deal of his work in secret, for he thought it was much better that his neighbors should know nothing of what he was doing.

So he looked for a workshop where no one would be likely to find him. He was now living in Strasburg, and there was in that city a ruined old building where, long before his time, a number of monks had lived. There was one room of the building which needed only a little repairing to make it fit to be used. So Gutenberg got the right to repair that room and use it as his workshop.

All his neighbors wondered what became of him when he left home in the early morning, and where he had been when they saw him coming back late in the twilight. Some felt sure that he must be a wizard, and that he had meetings somewhere with the devil, and that the devil was helping him to do some strange business.

Gutenberg did not care much what people had to say, and in his quiet room he patiently tried one experiment after another, often feeling very sad and discouraged day after day because his experiments did not succeed.

At last the time came when he had no money left. He went back to his old home, Mainz, and there met a rich goldsmith named Fust (or Faust).

Gutenberg told him how hard he had tried in Strasburg to find some way of making books cheaply, and how he had now no more money to carry on his experiments. Fust became greatly interested and gave Gutenberg what money he needed. But as the experiments did not at first succeed Fust lost patience. He quarreled with Gutenberg and said that he was doing nothing but spending money. At last he brought suit against him in the court, and the judge decided in favor of Fust. So everything in the world that Gutenberg had, even the tools with which he worked, came into Fust's possession.

2

But though he had lost his tools, Gutenberg had not lost his courage. And he had not lost all his friends. One of them had money, and he bought Gutenberg a new set of tools and hired a workshop for him. And now at last Gutenberg's hopes were fulfilled. First of all it is thought that he made types of hard wood. Each type was a little block with a single letter at one end. Such types were a great deal better than block letters. The block letters were fixed. They could not be taken out of the words of which they were parts. The new types were movable so they could be set up to print one page, then taken apart and set up again and again to print any number of pages.

But type made of wood did not always print the letters clearly and distinctly, so Gutenberg gave up wood types and tried metal types. Soon a Latin Bible was printed. It was in two volumes, each of which had three hundred pages, while each of the pages had forty-two lines. The letters were sharp and clear. They had been printed from movable types of metal.

3

The Dutch claim that Lorenz Coster, a native of Harlem, in the Netherlands, was the first person who printed with movable type. They say that Coster was one day taking a walk in a beech forest not far from Harlem, and that he cut bark from one of the trees and shaped it with his knife into letters.

Not long after this the Dutch say Coster had made movable types and was printing and selling books in Harlem.

The news that books were being printed in Mainz by Gutenberg went all over Europe, and before he died printing-presses like his were at work making books in all the great cities of the continent.

About twenty years after his death, when Venice was the richest of European cities, a man named Aldus (Al'-dus) Manutius (Ma-nu'-tius) established there the most famous printing house of that time. He was at work printing books two years before Columbus sailed on his first voyage. The descendents of Aldus continued the business after his death for about one hundred years. The books published by them were called "Aldine," from Aldus. They were the most beautiful that had ever come from the press. They are admired and valued to this day.

Fig. 18 – Gutenberg Bible, first printed book, owned by the US Library of Congress

Warwick the Kingmaker. Lived from 1428-1471

1

The earl of Warwick, known as the "kingmaker," was the most famous man in England for many years after the death of Henry V. He lived in a great castle with two towers higher than most church spires. It is one of the handsomest dwellings in the world and is visited every year by thousands of people. The kingmaker had a guard of six hundred men. At his house in London meals were served to so many people that six fat oxen were eaten at breakfast alone. He had a hundred and ten estates in different parts of England and no less than 30,000 persons were fed daily at his board. He owned the whole city of Worcester, and besides this and three islands, Jersey, Guernsey and Alderney, so famed in our time for their cattle, belonged to him.

He had a cousin of whom he was as fond as if he were a brother. This was Richard, duke of York, who was also own cousin to King Henry VI, the son of Henry V.

One evening as the sun was setting, and the warders were going to close the gates of the city of York for the night, a loud blast of a horn was heard. It was made by the sentry on the wall near the southern gate. An armed troop was approaching. When they drew near the gate their scarlet coats embroidered with the figure of a boar proved them to be the men of the earl of Warwick. The earl himself was behind them. The gate was opened.

Passing through it and on to the castle, the earl and his company were soon within its strong stone walls.

"Cousin," said the earl of Warwick to the duke of York as they sat talking before a huge log fire in the great room of the castle, "England will not long endure the misrule of a king who is half the time out of his mind."

The earl spoke the truth. Every now and then Henry VI lost his reason, and the duke of York, or some other nobleman, had to govern the kingdom for him.

The earl of Warwick added: "You are the rightful heir to the throne. The claim of Henry VI comes through Lancaster, the fourth son of Edward III--yours through Lionel, the second. His claim comes through his father only--yours through both your father and mother. It is a better claim and it is a double claim."

"That is true, my cousin of Warwick," replied the duke of York, "but we must not plunge England into war."

"Surely not if we can help it," replied the earl. "Let us first ask for reform. If the king heeds our petition, well and good. If not I am determined, cousin of York, that you shall sit on the throne of England instead of our insane sovereign."

A petition was soon drawn up and signed and presented to Henry. It asked that Henry would do something which would make the people contented.

The king paid no attention to it. Then a war began. It was the longest and most terrible that ever took place in England. It lasted for thirty years.

Those who fought on the king's side were called Lancastrians, because Henry's ancestor, John of Gaunt, was the duke of Lancaster. The friends of Richard were called Yorkists, because he was duke of York. The Lancastrians took a red rose for their badge; the Yorkists a white one. For this reason the long struggle has always been called the "War of the Roses."

In the first great battle the Red Rose party was defeated and the king himself was taken prisoner.

The victors now thought that the duke of York ought to be made king at once. However, a parliament was called to decide the question, and it was agreed that Henry should be king as long as he lived, but that at his death the crown should pass to the duke of York.

2

Most people though this was a wise arrangement; but Queen Margaret, Henry's wife, did not like it at all, because it took from her son the right to reign after his father's death. So she went to Scotland and the North of England, where she had many friends, and raised an army.

She was a brave woman and led her men in a battle in which she gained the victory. The duke of York was killed, and the queen ordered some of her men to cut off his head, put upon it a paper crown in mockery, and fix it over one of the gates of the city of York.

Warwick attacked the queen again as soon as he could; but again she was victorious and captured from Warwick her husband, the king, whom the earl had held prisoner for some time past.

This was a great triumph for Margaret, for Henry became king once more.

But the people were still discontented. The York party was determined that Edward, the son of the old duke of York, should be made king. So thousands flocked to the White Rose standard and Warwick marched to London at their head.

The queen saw that her only safety was in flight. She left London and the kingmaker entered the city in triumph.

The citizens had been very fond of the old duke of York, and when his party proclaimed his handsome young son King Edward IV, the city resounded with the cry "God save King Edward."

Brave Queen Margaret was completey defeated in another battle. The story is told that after this she fled into a forest with her young son. A robber met them, but Margaret, with wonderful courage, said to him, "I am your queen and this is your prince. I entrust him to your care."

The man was pleased with the confidence that she showed. He took her and the young prince to a safe hiding place, and helped them to escape from England in a sailing vessel.

3

Edward IV now seemed to be seated securely upon the throne. But trouble was near. Warwick wished him to follow his advice. Edward thought he could manage without any advice. Then the king and the kingmaker quarreled, and at last became open enemies and fought one another on the field of battle. The end of it was that Warwick was defeated, and driven out of the country. He sailed across the channel and sought refuge in France.

There whom should he meet but his old enemy, Queen Margaret. She had beaten him in battle, and had beheaded his cousin Richard, duke of York; he had beaten her and driven her from her kingdom; and twice he had made her husband prisoner and taken from him his crown. In spite of all this the two now became fast friends, and the kingmaker agreed to make war upon Edward and restore Henry to the throne.

He asked assistance from Louis XI, king of France, who supplied him with men and money. So with an army of Frenchmen the kingmaker landed on the shores of England. Thousands of Englishmen who were tired of Edward flocked to Warwick's standard, and when he reached London he had an army of sixty thousand men.

Edward fled without waiting for a battle and escaped to the Netherlands in a sailing-vessel. The kingmaker had now no one to resist him. The gates of London were opened to him, and the citizens heartily welcomed him. Marching to the Tower, he brought out the old king and placed him once more upon the throne.

But though Edward had fled, he was not discouraged. He followed the example of the kingmaker and asked aid from foreign friends. The duke of Burgundy supplied him with money and soldiers, and he was soon back in England.

His army grew larger and larger every day. People had been very much dissatisfied with Edward and had rejoiced to get rid of him and have Henry for king, because if Henry was not clever he was good. But in a short time they had found out that England needed a king who was not only good but capable.

So when Edward and his French soldiers landed most people in England welcomed them. The kingmaker was now on the wrong side.

Edward met him in battle at a place called Barnet, and completely defeated him. Warwick was killed and Henry once more became prisoner.

In another battle both Margaret and her son were made prisoners. The son was brutally murdered in the presence of King Edward. Margaret was placed in the Tower, and King Henry, who died soon after the battle of Tewksbury, was probably poisoned by order of Edward.

In 1438, after a reign of twenty-two years, Edward died, leaving two sons. Both were boys, so Edward's brother, Richard, duke of Gloucester, was made regent until young Edward V, the older of the two, should come of age.

But Richard was determined to make himself king. So he put both the young princes in the Tower. He than hired ruffians to murder them. One night, when the little princes were asleep, the murderers smothered them with pillows and buried their bodies at the foot of a stairway in the Tower, and there, after many years, their bones were found.

After Richard had murdered his two nephews, he was crowned king, as Richard III, much pleased that his plans had succeeded so well. He thought that now nobody could lay claim to the throne. But he was mistaken. One person did claim it. This was Henry Tudor, earl of Richmond.

Henry's father, Edmund Tudor, was only a Welsh gentleman, but was the half-brother of Henry VI through their mother Queen Katherine. Henry's mother was descended from John of Gaunt, fourth son of Edward III, and thus through his mother he was of royal blood and a Lancastrian.

When Richard III by his wickedness and cruelty had made all England hate him, the Red Rose party gathered about Henry Tudor, raised an army, and fought against the king in the battle of Bosworth.

Richard was a bad man, but he was brave, and he fought like a lion. However, it was all in vain. He was defeated and killed. His body was thrown on the back of a horse, carried to a church near the field of battle and buried.

The battered crown which Richard had worn was picked up and placed on Henry's head and the whole Lancastrian army shouted, "Long live King Henry!"

Parliament now voted that Henry Tudor and his heirs should be kings of England. Not long afterwards Henry married the heiress of the house of York, and thus both the Red Roses and the White were satisfied, as the king was a Lancastrian and the queen a Yorkist.

So the long and terrible Wars of the Roses came to an end.

Made in the USA
Las Vegas, NV
13 July 2022